HOW TO FIND FULFILLMENT BY LETTING YOURSELF FAIL

THE JOURNEY TO FAILING FREELY

Brandon LaBella

The Journey To Failing Freely
Copyright © 2018 by Brandon LaBella

No part of this publication may be reproduced, distributed, or transmitted in any form or by any means, including photocopying, recording, or other electronic or mechanical methods, without the prior written permission of the author, except in the case of brief quotations embodied in critical reviews and certain other non-commercial uses permitted by copyright law.

tellwell

Tellwell Talent
www.tellwell.ca

ISBN
978-1-77370-667-2 (Paperback)
Printed in Canada

TABLE OF CONTENTS

Dedication 5
Acknowledgements 7
Foreword 9
Introduction 17

Part 1 -> Numb On Auto-Pilot 25

Chapter 1 -> The Yellow Brick Road Fleece 27
Chapter 2-> Comfortably Numb 35
Chapter 3-> Craving Makes Us Weak 51

Part 2-> The Mindset Movement To Wake Up 63

Chapter 4-> Striking Out With Pleasure 65
Chapter 5-> Renatus 77

Part 3-> Failing Up 87

Chapter 6 -> Ask the Right Questions 89
Chapter 7 -> Break Free of the Chains 101
Chapter 8 -> Build a New Toolbox to Maintain Growth 111
Chapter 9 -> How to Fail Freely 125

Conclusion 141
About the Author 149

DEDICATION

Herrington Bryce and Jean Bellemans
PC- CGOD
To Sarah, Keep Living Free and Fulfilled
To Trent, Thank You for Not Having the
South African Police Called on Me
Enrico, Mario, and Nico -> Remember
Every Day "It's Going to Be Ok"
To my Parents -> Thanks for letting
me be free and fulfilled
To Gianna-> Can't Wait to Climb Mount
Chimborazo with You and Fail Freely Again
To my Friends-> Thanks for allowing me to
be myself and all of the amazing support
Dawn and Jolynn -> Thanks for the Inspiration.
Please Don't Please Too Many People.
Gary M and Fraser-Ill see you at top
Fam ☺ or asleep at Eleven.
Mikey G-> Day 1 Tides Have Turned
Bryan-> You are amazing!
Ben-> I'll be there at mile 9 for you
when you start your podcast
Dom-> Every day is so beautiful
push the rock up every day.
PJ + Hank -> Rue Charles Degroux ETF Barca Boys
for Life. Thanks For Saving My Life Multiple Times
To those I have strangled freedom from -> I hope
this book makes you freer and fulfilled
To those who are struggling and suffering ->
You can start your journey tomorrow!

ACKNOWLEDGEMENTS

I was tired of being told by everyone around me I was doing great and on the right path when I hadn't failed once and felt caged on a societal leash. So, I went inside myself, read my own book and understood what I wanted. It was time for someone in college to do something to make others more aware of how to go through this life with the freedom of being alive it deserves through themselves before it was too late. So, this book goes inside my change from doing everything to please other people to finding myself and gives you the actionable steps to go inside yourself and do the same. I am excited for you to begin this journey and start your flight to fulfillment. I truly believe our assumptions about the world continue to drift further from the truth. In order to find the truth, you need to have life experiences and **go out and do things.** Stop seeking the answers from the infinite knowledge base of the internet and start seeking answers about yourself.

I can't truly describe in words the amount of epic experiences and epic people that I have been lucky enough to meet throughout my journey this past year that you have the power to experience if you start your journey. There are too many people in my 2016 shoes living a life restricted by trying preserve a self-image that isn't even their true authentic self. There are too many people becoming the best possible version of someone else, unintentionally strangling their own and others freedom. There are too many people using vices to hide problems that are drifting ourselves further away from solving problems that we have the ability to overcome and move forward tomorrow to make the world a healthier place. The underlying issue I have with these fixable issues is that it limits us from what we can achieve, and not achieving our full potential is going to stop us from our dreams, which is going to leave us looking back asking "What If" with regrets and unfulfillment. I can't wait to see everyone who reads this book on the top of their own mountain spreading their fulfilled wings fueling others to chase their own freedom and fulfillment! The author of this book is **YOU**. This book isn't called "Be the Best Possible Version of Brandon!" I am not replicable. And Neither Is Your Beautiful Self! Thank you Madison for sifting through my non-sense stories and finding some way to organize my writing so it could reach the most amount of people. We had a 1 and 4 billion chance of being born into this beautiful world, make it count. Capitals Are Scattered Throughout The Text To Remind You To Treat Everyone With Love

FOREWORD

Dawn Edmiston

When I arrived at the College of William & Mary in the fall of 2014, I was thrilled to join one of the leading "Public Ivies" in the U.S. However, I had not expected during my first two weeks on campus that I would receive more meeting requests from students to discuss their mental health issues than their career aspirations. At the end of that academic year, there had been four suicides on campus. For a college that prides itself on being a very close-knit community (in fact, we refer to ourselves as the "Tribe"), we were shattered and heartbroken, wondering how we could prevent such tragic loss in the future.

Brandon LaBella and this book are truly part of the answer.

It was obvious when Brandon arrived in my marketing class in the fall of 2017 that he was forging a different path than most of my students. During our first meeting, we spent the first few minutes as expected, talking about his previous work experience and his impending graduation at the end of the semester. However, when I asked Brandon about his recent travels, there was an immediate shift in the conversation. Brandon's eyes lit up and his speech quickened as if he wanted to make sure to have enough time to share every life-changing encounter with me. At that moment, he became the teacher and I became the student who was transformed by his joie de vivre.

As we continued our meetings during the semester (typically via Skype as Brandon explored the world), he began to share with me his concepts for this book to include the power of positivity and "failing freely." I immediately recognized these were messages that every single one of my college students needed to hear. Because at the College of William & Mary we do not simply have "Type A" personalities, we have "Type AA" personalities. I am surrounded by students who are both inspired and inspiring. However, they too often feel the superficial pressures of the world around them and measure success by society's yardstick not their own. And, honestly, that is how I felt in college as well.

We live in a world that emphasizes consumerism rather than community, and values the notion of success higher than the virtue of service. Brandon's personal narrative about how he overcame the notion of being on auto-pilot in college and learned the value of taking risks is more important than any academic textbook and should be required reading for all college students. Brandon's words motivate us to be compassionate humans and thoughtful individuals that share a love for life … and for each other.

As a marketing professor, I will admit that sometimes I am desperately at odds with the notions of consumerism and commercialization that my discipline seems to propagate. Gratitude and grace are typically not found in advertising campaigns. However, as a marketer, I do understand the power of communication. And I do believe that each of us has the power to use our words and actions to contribute to a greater good. Brandon's words and actions serve as a role model for his generation ... and give me such hope for our future.

Dawn Edmiston January 2018
Clinical Associate Professor @ William and Mary

Shane Breslin

Brandon LaBella and I never been in the same room before, but the 3000 miles that separate us have not put any boundaries between the freedom that is created through the power of technology.

When we started, we found it hard to stop.

One video call, when he or I or both of us were under enough time pressure to agree to a 15-minute limit, we were still talking 45 minutes later.

Whatever it was that we needed to do, we needed to talk more.

What might be the common ground between a 40-year-old Irishman who has been through a handful of careers and industries and has only recently learned to embrace the uncertainty that comes with every day, and a 22-year-old from New York who is, in so many ways, just starting out on his own journey?

I could make it complicated - people can make anything complicated, if we just hang around with it for a while - but for us it's fairly simple. We're both interested in helping people be happier, healthier, with fuller lives.

There is a crisis right now in the western world. It's a crisis of confidence, a crisis of wellbeing, of health, of fulfilment. It's a crisis of happiness.

By all cold economic measures, if you look at things in the developed world objectively, things have rarely been better.

Life expectancy is at an all-time high. Infant mortality is at an all-time low. We live in societies where, for the most part, almost everyone has the basic needs of food, warmth and shelter, and tens of thousands of charitable people all over the world are dedicated selflessly to helping the unfortunate few who find themselves temporarily without those comforts.

So why then are we so unhappy?

Why is 1 in every 12 adults in the US and Ireland and Canada and the UK and western Europe suffering from depression at any given time?

Why is another 1 in 12 suffering from anxiety?

Why is treatment that works so readily available when our arm is broken, but only 1 in 3 people whose mind is broken find themselves with the necessary supports?

Why has there been a 300 percent rise in the consumption of antidepressants over the past 30 years?

Why are people so rapidly encouraged to pop a pill when it is scientifically proven that non-medical treatments such as cognitive behavioral therapy has *better long-term results without any dependency or side-effects*?

And why, why, why does the exponential rise coincide with *increased* rates of depression, anxiety and a host of related disorders?

There is little doubt that something is broken in the way so many of us look at ourselves as human beings, in the way so many of us behave towards ourselves, in the way so many of us talk to ourselves in a way we would never talk to another human being.

The solution?

This world and everything in it is filled with so much uncertainty, but what I'm about to say, I say with the most absolute certainty I've ever had about anything.

The long-term solution does not come in the form of a pill.

It comes in the form of our small positive choices.

It turns out the knock-on effects of one small positive choice, when we can find the strength in ourselves and the support from others to turn that small positive choice into a small positive habit, will change your life.

And here's something that might blow your mind.

That small positive habit will not just change your life.

The domino fall that a small positive habit sets in motion will change the life of everyone close to you.

And it can change the life of one or two or dozens or hundreds or millions of people who you don't even know.

The world is a still pond, and your small positive choice can start a ripple that might never stop.

I know, because that is my story.

Two years ago, I hit rock bottom after two decades of depression. Depression cost me three jobs in fine organizations in totally different industries. It almost cost me my home. It almost cost me my marriage.

When I made the small positive choice of talking about depression, and talking about taking on the challenge of depression openly and honestly, when I wanted to find a solution rather than a temporary sticking plaster, I found so much strength in areas that others might have seen as total weakness.

The small ripples started, and long may they continue outward.

For the last portion of this journey, Brandon and I have been regular correspondents.

We share a conviction that one person's positive mental health has far-reaching benefits for *everything*, in their body, in their relationships and in their impact on the world.

We share a conviction that every single one of us has the power to make our corner of the world a better place.

I am hugely honored to be a small part of this book, I am inspired by Brandon as I know everyone who reads this book will be and I am excited to see the scale of the legacy this young man from New York will leave on the wider world in the decades to come.

Shane Breslin
January 2018

INTRODUCTION

It was sunrise on the last day of December 2017. The sky was filled with ruby grapefruit and mandarin orange tones at Playland Park in Rye, NY. Steam rose into the air from my blue full facial mask hidden behind my red Beats with a missing logo on my left ear.

12 hours later, sweat dripped down my striped polo shirt and tight black soccer pants, as I desperately tried to find my way to the hostel where I'd be spending the night.

"Bonsui, we only have manual" said the saleswoman at EuropCar at the Guadeloupe Airport in the French Caribbean. I thought to myself that it was the perfect challenge to end the year. I had four hours to get to the Butterfly Hostel before the clock hit midnight. To my dismay, learning how to drive a stick would not be an accomplishment of 2017. Instead, I found an automatic at Jumbocar, and easily made it to my destination thanks to the "Waze" app. If only I was cruising on automatic the other 364 days of the year. My life would have been so easy and boring, and I would have inspired no one.

Rather, I failed at least 122 times and counting in 2017, and embarked on an uncomfortable journey that has helped me find true sustainable happiness through freedom and fulfillment over short-term pleasure. I stopped caring about what other people thought, and took full control of living a limitless life with endless possibilities. For the first 364 days of the year, I was in manual mode. Whether it was saving two blacked out girls on ATVs in Mykonos, hanging off a cliff in a cold misty day on Table Mountain in South Africa, getting breathalyzed near the Margaret River in Australia, graduating college, or crossing the finish line at the NYC Marathon with two crutches as a world record holder, I deserved day 365 to be on automatic.

The reality of life is that things don't always work out the way we want them to. I can't remember the last time when something worked out the way I planned it. I thought that after training for the NYC Marathon for months without drinking alcohol and healthy eating, I would be able to cross the finish line under 3 hours and 30 minutes, having raised over $3,000 to support Pencils of Promise. I thought I'd get a nice picture of myself crossing the finish line and get a ton of likes on Instagram. But that changed in a heartbeat when I went in for a slide tackle in my indoor soccer semi-final playoff game. In that one moment, I sprained my MCL *and* ACL. It would have been so easy for me to complain and give up. But as I sat there in pain, wondering how I was going to tell everyone that I couldn't run the marathon, I told myself that I wasn't giving up. I had to give it everything I had without harming my knee further.

And with that one decision, I broke the Guinness world record for fastest marathon ever on crutches at 6 hours, 19 minutes in the New York City Marathon. I told myself if I tried for one mile and it didn't workout, that would have been just as great a success as I would have inspired the other runners by giving them an extra motivational push. The accomplishment of completing the marathon on crutches felt good, don't get me wrong, but for me it was about the intention and the journey of training for the marathon, not the finish line.

In a lot of ways, life is just like that marathon. It takes discipline, hard work, patience, good habits, and TIME. But inch-by-inch, mile-by-mile, you can cross the finish line feeling free and fulfilled every day. Whether you are a billionaire with multiple yachts in Italy or a homeless man in South Africa, it is possible to achieve freedom and fulfillment because we are all born with the ability to fail. The ability to fail is the root of freedom, fulfillment, and happiness. If you create small wins every day, you are going to live a life full of sustainable fulfillment - and one with the freedom you deserve. Because at the end of the day, our life can be over in a snap. And the only thing you have to show is the legacy of freedom and fulfillment you've created for yourself and others.

The hardest part is starting the race. Just like the hardest part for me was the anticipation of starting that marathon. I received concerned emails and phone calls from my donors strongly advising me to not even attempt it the night before.

"Forget about it and move on to the next one, when you're healthy." I greatly respected these people. But I knew I couldn't live with myself without stepping foot at the start of the race. That's all I could ask of myself. That's the danger you are facing today in your life. Many of us will never start our journey to freeing ourselves. Constant external noise will take you down a black hole that will restrict you from setting foot at the starting line of being your authentic self. Fear and comfort are only going to starve your dreams from coming true.

I have truly found the freedom of a little kid in a candy shop every day, without sugar. It all started with changing my habits, creating beliefs about who I wanted to become, becoming a master of my beliefs and mantras, and celebrating those beliefs everyday by feeling alive and free in the present. Every day I wake up with a smile on my face, drink a glass of water and journal about how thankful I am to be alive. The rest of my day is spontaneous but allows me to enjoy activities like exercise, adventure, and meaningful conversations with awesome people. I found my purpose and it is this: to use my enthusiasm and determination to motivate and inspire others to live every day fulfilled, mentally and physically healthy, and feel the freedom of experiencing being alive with their authentic self every day. I define authentic self as being the best possible version of yourself with what you control moving forward on your own journey. This is because our being is a process and we can either grow every day with courage and gratitude to improve ourselves and those around us, or make excuses, avoid our problems by numbing out, and move backwards dragging other people with us. The latter I would define as being the weakest possible version of our inauthentic self. That state is old, fake news. We are in the present my friends and the only way is up! If you are still struggling with this concept, ask yourself if tomorrow was your last day, how would you spend it? Just like starting the journey, it's up to you ;) I am here to teach others how to free themselves, find their purpose, and give themselves a chance to fail.

I've traveled to 36 countries in my life, and my experiences have truly made me appreciate the opportunities that we have been given in America. Even though the U.S. is often criticized as a materialistic society, people all over the world would do anything to move here and chase the so-called American Dream. But, based on my experiences, it is evident to me that freedom and fulfillment are things we are failing at due to the mindset we have cultivated in our society. It is sucking the freedom out of us, one-by-one. If we don't go within ourselves and create freedom for ourselves and others moving forward, this so called American Dream will turn into the American Nightmare.

This has created a mental health and opioid crisis that continues to spiral out of control. But I couldn't be more excited about how this is going to change for the better in 2018 and beyond. There is so much healthy content to consume, and more resources available to us than ever before. As I wished a Happy New Year to people in the French Caribbean in the beginning of January, I tried to add a positive note to our conversation, "This is going to be the best year of our lives, are you excited?!" Those who understood me have responded with a laugh and something along the lines of, "Every year is the same."

But I would beg to differ, with love. I truly believe this book will shift your entire mindset about each year moving forward in a positive, freeing way!

So why I am I trying to thrust freedom upon you? What does living a sustainable, free life even mean? I am devastated to see all the people who work so hard, have it all, yet are enslaved and unfulfilled in "the real world" only to realize money, job title, and material things deprive them from enjoying the journey, make them feel empty, and restrict them from finding peace with their healthy authentic selves. There are so many unnecessary times that we stress, worry, inflict pain on other people, and create negativity for ourselves in a world that we are all going to die in. For me, freedom is a moment in time where we are able to live in the present without any restrictions or stresses, and without harming others. For me, that means not having any fears about my self-image or chilling with my good buddy and our two stuffed animals in pajamas playing Madden 2004 with no worries in the world. Fulfillment for me means creating purpose for myself and other people by inspiring others and myself to wake up each morning with the intention to become the best possible version of our authentic self rather than best version of someone who we are not. Fulfillment comes from overcoming obstacles and meaningful relationships. Or, in other words, having a meaningful conversation with my buddy at 6 am about how he has crushed his goals for the month, inspiring both of us to grow and improve even more for the upcoming month. Afterward, crushing a sunrise workout consisting of stretching, yoga, sprints, a gallon of Poland spring water, and tossing the football around talking about how we are going to crush the day. Then, writing down what I am thankful for in my gratitude journal while feasting on a grilled chicken avocado egg white omelet with Dave's Killer Bread toasted crispy. I call this kind of fulfillment "FreeFillment," because it not only allows you to free yourself of your baggage, but it creates lasting happiness every day. It's like a drug that - once taken - never lets you go back to your old way of thinking. You can never go back to how things were. The symptoms of the FreeFilled drug include being yourself, being in control, being healthy both physically and mentally, and having the ability to grow and improve each day you're lucky enough to be alive. Because there is always going to be another mountain, another problem, another person who seems like they are happier and better than you, but if you're free and following your purpose, none of that matters.

Although it is not going to be a quick fix, I am writing this book to create eternal freedom and fulfillment in your life through sustainable, authentic pleasure. You have everything you need to start your journey right now. You are worthy, and you have a gift that will impact the world. If you don't start your journey now, chances are you will never start it, and that would be doing a big disservice to yourself and the world around you. Because you are depriving others from growing and learning from you. My biggest fear is that you will waste all the talent and gifts you were born carrying into this world. And to me that would be the saddest waste of talent.

I dream of a world in which we can all put aside our differences and wake up every day as free as a little kid, enjoying the feeling of being alive in each present moment to the best of our ability. I dream that we all feel free rather than strangled and hindered by ourselves and others. It's time to pull the trigger and book your flight to freedom and fulfillment - right now! You *can* live forever young like the good old days, freely in control, but only if you commit to failing up.

What's at Stake?

When Starting Your Journey of Life You Are Guaranteed to Fail, But We Continue to Go Down The Wrong Path (Failing Down), which includes unintentionally harming other people and making them feel unworthy at the expense of finding ourselves.

Brandon advocates the concepts of Failing Up as:

- Taking Calculated Risks When You Are Physically and Mentally Healthy Feeling Awake
- Embracing The Pain of Suffering
- Putting Yourself In Safe Environments to Grow While Reaching Your Full Potential
- Living a Life Without Regrets

This would be defined as Failing Freely, Being Yourself and Waking Up Each Day Being Your Authentic Self.

Rather Than Failing Down, Taking Uncalculated Risks When You are Not Mentally And Physically Healthy a.k.a. When You Are Unconscious, Unawake, Numbing Out Pain through Substances While Making Others Feel Unworthy, and Ultimately Not Reaching Your Full Potential and Living Life With Regrets.

This would be defined as Failing Unwisely, Being The Best Possible Version of Who You Are Not.

You Are Beautiful and Were Born With The Ability To Fail Freely :)

PART 1: Enslaved On Auto-Pilot

Before You Start Your Journey, Send a Picture of This To Someone Who You Care About Who You Haven't Talked To In A While

Life is a journey

Each of us has a story

I send this little note today to show you that I care.

While we may not always have a daily conversation,

You left me with a reminder that I carry in my heart to this very day.

Because when I think of you, I want to you know you are special to me.

You have positively impacted me and left me a better person than before we met.

I hope that I have made you feel the same way and it is my hope that we will talk again some day.

Live Every Day Like You Will Die Tomorrow,

Learn Every Day Like You Will Live Forever,

Never Stop Believing In Yourself

You Are Worthy and Awesome <3

Don't Stop Being Yourself. You Are Beautiful and Irreplaceable the Way You Are.

CHAPTER 1

THE YELLOW BRICK ROAD FLEECE

"How society tells us to live?"

One of the biggest misunderstandings that I got caught up in before starting my journey is feeling like I had to blindly run down the path I was given. For me, I fell into the trap of falling into the autopilot of society's expectations for me. That's why I want to share my story: to make sure you get to create your own expectations and you don't sell your soul away to some predetermined idea that you've been told is the "right" way to live.

Look, I get it. It sounds pretty cool to be "Popping pills and fucking hoes like a rock star" with Post Malone, or doing "Mali and Percocet" with Future. Until my parents rewarded me for middle school graduation with a ruby raspberry LG2 flip phone, I had absolutely no clue what was going on in the world. My parents were quite protective of me and always demonstrated the need to read and work hard. But they, and any other parent in my hometown, didn't have any idea how to prepare their kids for the social aspect of high school I embarked on. Looking back, it was frightening how asleep I was for someone who had an amazing support network of parents, teachers, and friends in the town I was raised.

In high school, I tried to follow everyone who was "socially cool" and be like them. I didn't know any better, and at that age I was not aware of any options to enjoy myself outside of sports. So, when I started getting into activities and participating in groups, it was inevitable I'd find a seemingly-nice friend to introduce me to alcohol or drugs.

I remember the first time I started my journey with alcohol. It was April Fool's day and I was with three of my buddies at the time when we decided to get drunk. Pete and I ended up playing 1-on-1 basketball and I distinctly remember chucking up an air ball and laughing so hard I fell to the floor feeling like a kid enjoying the moment. I also remember Pete's Dad's speech at the annual hike we do in remembrance of his son after he overdosed. There are always positives to take out of negative situations. When you lose someone close to you, it is important to understand that the pain is caused by the enjoyment of having that person in your life. The pain is present because you have been so lucky to experience that person. And we were all lucky to experience Pete. His laugh and smile always contagiously spread to those around him. Same thing with Pete's best friend from elementary school. Contagious laugh and smile, loved by everyone in the community, really good at sports, and brilliant in the classroom at Vanderbilt. The list of amazing people who have passed too young can go on and on. Pete, Elliot, and myself fell helplessly into pleasure culture and spreading that same mentality to those around us. Thankfully Pete and Elliot passed free and fulfilled besides the fact that those we looked up to in our society passed the same mentality that I was passed down into "Maintain very high grades in school, and whenever you aren't doing that, get fucked up." That's all I heard when I arrived at school and it sounded like the dream to me at the time.

Going into high school as an innocent high schooler and college student, no advice my parents or teachers told me would have gotten in my way of trying to be socially cool. I was truly helpless understanding who was the best person to follow and what communities I should join. I used to think it was the cool thing to do to follow whatever someone else was doing because he had that dream job or he was gratified as a "legend or cool kid." I wanted to please those types of people by doing whatever they were doing even if it was bad for my health. The same thing happened on the opposite end. When people started looking up to me as a role model, they started doing whatever it took to please me which definitely didn't fit their values and they also couldn't emulate my system that worked only for my unique, beautiful self. I was not properly educated on how to look up to people older than me or teach people younger than me until I work. This mindset starved the freedom of myself by being someone who I was not, while making others chasing after something they were not.

Each year starting in 2011, I would use this mindset to continue to move up society's ladder and nothing had changed in 2012, 2013, 2014, 2015, and 2016. I couldn't let 2017 be the same: walking blindly down the imaginary yellow brick road to "success." The only reason why 2017 was different was because I got free from my comfort leash and gave myself the chance to fail.

I pulled the trigger and embarked on my own journey to steer clear of that yellow brick road. That road sucked me in so subtly I didn't even notice, starving my freedom and those around me even though I felt on top of the world and truly believed I was helping those who I was lucky enough to have in my life. It is time for you to start your journey too. Freeing yourself and those around you - unless you want to wake up in 2028 with the last 10 years being a blur and feeling exactly as stuck as you do now. Those years could be defined as chasing the Invisible Summit on Auto-Pilot Blinded by Fear and Comfort. Or you could decide to make a change. To take off your blinders and start your journey right now to Failing Up. I promise you that if you start this journey today and pull the trigger, you will freely fail in 2018.

How Do We Set Our Bright, Beloved Middle School, High School, and College Students Down The Free Path?

I truly believe we need to redefine what socially cool means and have an open, authentic discussion about how to make the weekends more beneficial to our own lives and those suffering around the world. The current college and high school students are open as ever to make a change in the world. Many would do anything in the world to help others. I was the same way in college. I loved helping people, participating in charity activities, and venmoing friends who were raising awareness and money for good causes. Call me whatever you want at the time, lazy, selfish, undisciplined, but the truth is that if we really want to change the "Going Out Culture", we need to provide an option that is as easy to participate in as an amazon one click checkout and as gratifying as snapping a picture of a glass of wine at a sunset that positively impacts the world. We need to make it easier for these bright young stars to participate in accessible, rewarding overnight hikes, provide accessible entertaining environments to learn how to dance while meeting new people in environments, provide fun games around photography, writing, and creating music, create community wide board game competitions around Jenga, Scrabble, and all the other games. And lastly and most importantly, we need to have influencers and celebrities educating our future on how to live life on the weekends while being a functional human being and create posts about how to enjoy life without substances, bottle service, and exclusive clubs. With the amount of followers of celebrities reaching 100 million, we truly have the power to set any standard of socially cool and help the next generation avoid FOMO of popping pills, blacking out, and consuming alcohol and drugs in the coolest way possible. It sounds stupid, but it is truly remarkable how shitty and alone you can feel reading a book on a Saturday night when you watch a celebrity making concoctions of fruit loops with Grey Goose as dinner for the pre-game, watching a millionaire doing drugs with 10 girls in bikini's around him, or viewing a youtube video with millions of views that contains lavish parties and large blunts getting passed around. I am not complaining, but rather shedding light and educating the population on what it takes to shift the "Socially Cool" Mindset and educate people on how to properly use social media. Because I got consumed by this mindset, I would immediately need to post and share pictures of me out at parties smiling twisted on drugs and alcohol. The reality is that although I thought it was cool and got a lot of likes, who was I truly helping? All I was doing was strangling freedom from others to make them think it was socially cool to drift further and further apart from their authentic selves. I truly don't really care what these celebrities and influencers do to be honest. I will be happy if they are having a good time enjoying life the way they want to live. But if they going to do that, I prefer they don't post on social media so that they don't strangle the freedom and improperly educate millions of people on how to live it up on a Friday and Saturday Night by numbing themselves out. I would much rather prefer them providing positive content that motivates and mentors people. I would much rather prefer them providing opportunities for their fans to do a cool activity on the weekends that involves donating to others, doing activities to raise money for charity, and being pioneers for being purposeful role models that make the world a better place by providing opportunities for the youth to grow and improve themselves through meaningful enjoyable activities.

The Mindset Shift?

While there are definitely lessons that can be learned from my past that were not role model worthy, it is really important to understand four things when you are learning from a role model good or bad.

1. Just because they check a box that you want to check, doesn't mean you should follow their lead
2. Just because there are things you want to emulate about a specific person, doesn't mean you should try to become them.
3. Just because you are happy being yourself and are crushing it, doesn't mean that same formula will work for someone else you are mentoring.
4. Don't Set Others Up To Feel Unworthy at the expense of Finding Yourself

My biggest advice to those in high school and college to completely crush "society's success metric" is to get uncomfortable with people and engage in experiences in safe environments that allow you to feel fully alive and fulfilled in the present moment and create opportunities within your network to get closer to finding your own spark and who you want to be. You know your beautiful self more than anyone and a true friend would want you to make a decision for yourself rather than please them.

CHAPTER 2:

COMFORTABLY NUMB

"How do we numb out?"

732 million views later on YouTube, Linkin Park's song "Numb" has become an icon to remember the legend of Chester Bennington. But while the views and the outpouring of love given to him has most definitely been appreciated, I would argue he is not impressed with the numbness of our current society to the blind pressure we face to go down someone else's path, rather than being ourselves. As he lies free and fulfilled in California, a majority of you lie "Numb" asleep in your autopilot world. It's not your fault. I was in your shoes a year ago chasing a path that was externally gratifying but left me blindly chasing an invisible summit I was helplessly thrust into.

On December 31st, 2016, I was prepared for college graduation the next year. Ever since I stepped into Ms. Singer's Kindergarten class with my navy-blue New York Yankees triangular brim hat and a charming smile, my mom and dad were cheering me on for my graduation date. They were going to be so proud! I was ready to face the world head-on and overcome everyone's negative comments like, "Don't graduate. The Real World sucks."

But only until I returned from a trip to Israel, Greece, Italy, South Africa, Dubai, Australia, and New Zealand did I wake up and realize I was completely unfree, chasing cheap thrills blindly. I finally had time for once in my life to get away from the auto-pilot mode that has plagued me since practicing for the SAT in my sophomore year of high school. The tricky part is that there are so many of us externally "crushing it" with many people admiring us we wouldn't even know; however, the positive external signals actually stagnate our motivation, growth, and hide the leash under which our freedom is enslaved.

The issue is not with the corporate world or the beautiful society we were born into. The issue is that I internally created a mindset that enslaved myself to pleasing other people, focusing on the next destination, being comfortable, and fearing failure. If you live this way, you will never be fulfilled and you will be completely replaceable. Everyone who looks up to you will never be fulfilled either. And they will create someone on a leash below them because of the guy who passed down "wisdom" to you. Let's call this the unintentional false happiness loop.

In January 2017, I had just gotten a perfect review from my manager at IBM, only to get rejected by multiple companies for positions that I qualified for and would have excelled at. But this was the best thing that ever happened to me. I learned at that moment that the only thing in my control was being my unique self -- being physically and mentally healthy, growing and improving every day, appreciating the present moment with people who allow me to be myself without harming others.

Not only did rejection motivate me, but it also made me look within myself and change my whole perspective that I had been helplessly taught by those crushing it in the external world. That perspective was also strangling me and whatever freedom I'd been born with. Wherever you are today, rejection will only make you stronger and freer, and you can't get rejected unless you give yourself a chance to fail. Embracing the freedom to fail has changed my life.

Checking Off Point B

Everyone wants to get from Point A to Point B. But the reality of the situation is that we don't know what Point B means. And that's why we will never be satisfied when we get there. Life wouldn't be enjoyable if we could just pop a Xanax and wake up at Point B. Point B is the India Venster route at Table Mountain South Africa. A steep downward cliff of faded gold yellow footsteps that make you think you are on the right path to the bottom, but when you get there you're hanging off a steep cliff, only to find out the path leads to a cloud of air with the Indian Ocean 500 feet below. That's what I was facing an hour into my downward descent, but it was a spot-on comparison to my life in a nutshell. The way I look at it, if you are alive and reading this book today, you are at basecamp right now, searching for the right path to get to an invisible finish line. Society makes you think you are chasing something that has a magical end to it by enslaving you to conform to its own expectations. In this present moment, you are Sisyphus.

Let me fill you in for a minute: According to Greek Mythology, Sisyphus chained himself to Death to protect himself, but when he did, he was punished by Hades for this act. His punishment was to roll a huge stone to the top of a mountain every day, only to find out that no matter how much effort he put into it, it would fall back down. The 99.9% who haven't started the journey are in Sisyphus' shoes, as they work so hard every day to accomplish nothing but more enslavement and unfulfillment.

The reality of the situation is that there is no summit in life. This is why no matter what stage we are climbing up the mountain, it is important to live it through your own lens. Whether you are 25, 42 or 68, you will always ask yourself, "What is the next step?" And if you continue to live like you are chasing the summit society portrays, you will be left unfulfilled. Destinations are overrated.

My idea of the summit is enjoying the journey every day I am lucky enough to wake up surrounded by amazing people, abiding by my values, and maximizing the freedom I have for myself and others each day.

My idea of being socially cool is taking action to impress yourself through being you and climbing up your own summit that you have created for yourself every day with baby step improvements. While you may get an urge to stuff your face with watermelon sour patches, binge watch netflix for 12 hours, or black out with substances when problems arise, numbing out to further avoid your pain will only strangle fulfillment potential later on your journey.

Recognizing the beauty of pain being your authentic self will only improve fulfillment and make the journey sweeter later in life.

I spent 12 months training for the marathon of life, and as a result I have created world class freedom and fulfillment for myself. Once you cross the finish line in the marathon of life, you enjoy each day being yourself, not harming others, physically and mentally healthy, and improving and growing every day with your foot in control of the gas pedal on this amazing journey of life.

Pleasing People

We all want to make a lot of money, have purpose in our jobs, change the world, bla bla bla bla, but checking the boxes could not put you further from that. Checking the boxes and paying the bills are mandatory to become physically and mentally healthy, but the in between time before the next box is checked off is backstabber to moving forward on the journey. With technology and cheap thrills being really accessible, it is easy to get into a mindset that will allow you to enjoy the journey in the short-term with pleasure and cheap thrills. Our present mindset on enjoying the journey is fake news. I would define enjoying the journey as having fulfilling, meaningful interactive experiences with yourself and others to create sustainable happiness. Rather than asking yourself how can I most and cheaply numb myself out until the next box is checked, lets shift the question to "What can I do today that will allow me to get to where I want to be in 5-10 years?" The in between checking boxes time is going to define whether you are going to move backwards or forwards on your summit to your own mountain. They are critical to helping you find your purpose. It's up to you how you want to spend this time, but the only facts I can give you on the matter is that you will feel emptier and emptier the more screen and substances you engage in to take time away from you. Finding enjoyment and meaning at the same time through activities with other likeminded people have proved to me it is possible to find true thrills. I have used intentionality and mindfulness to create boundaries to make sure I am doing everything for myself rather than other people. By reflecting on my energy levels, I can determine when I will happily eat honey wheat pretzels and go skiing to take the day off from work or be uncomfortably exploring the world meeting countless people taking pictures and cherishing each moment I am doing me and not anyone else. Getting uncomfortable through unique activities with people you have never met before such as salsa, ballet, jiujitsu, public speaking, or photography are one of the thousand of options where you can meet other amazing people, learn how to ask questions, and get a temporary feeling of being alone and lost. Going against the grain in this safe environment will open up your curiosity and help you get closer to your true self while making you curious and motivated! It's only going to make you please more people in a comfortable state. I could never say no because I didn't want to harm someone on the receiving end of a no. I could never say no because I wouldn't have known what to do with myself if I didn't have a constant stream of plans with different people running around each day. I thrived and enjoyed it. However, internally I was doing a disservice to myself because saying yes was avoiding my fears. I couldn't stand alone for a second by myself without complaining or getting bored. The weekends were even better. I couldn't go out with my friends unless I drank, because I was uncomfortable talking to people when I was sober. Saying yes leads to avoidance of failure to check boxes that pile layers of comfort of security into our life. When I hung out with my particular tribe of friends, it wasn't any easier to fail. My friends were so good at enjoying life and being there for each other that we created an atmosphere where failing wasn't really an option. I admire all of them, but I realized that I wasn't going to grow unless I became uncomfortable and resisted the urge to take the easy route. I started to say no to any activity that wasn't a "Jumping Out of My Seat Yes" and replacing that time to find myself. I would still would kick it back with them occasionally to watch sports and infuse positivity into the crew with intentional enjoyment and comfort. Even with hanging out with my friends, it was astonishing how much free time I had when I wasn't going out. It's scary at the beginning how poor my time management was because my auto-pilot life would either be grinding at school or going out with friends. This free time ended up being the biggest blessing in disguise, because it allowed me to understand what I would do if there were no band-aids to pass time, by answering this question

> How would you spend your 56-hour weekend if all alcohol, drugs, and gambling were banned tomorrow? How would you maximize it for your enjoyment?

This is when I woke up and realized I was 100% enslaved in control chasing cheap thrills blindly. I realized that my definition of enjoying the journey did not fall under the types of situations I was saying yes to. I wasn't spending enough time on personal development, I wasn't getting enough sleep, I was harming my body, I was wasting my valuable time, and stagnating my growth just to please others. At first, saying no was tough because it's easy to get FOMO by not being at a bar or party, but I realized there was nothing better than enjoying the journey and feeling on top of the world pleasing myself. No checked-box, substance, or number of likes could beat that. Rather, spontaneously living a slow and fulfilling life prepared me to embrace any experience that called my name. And most importantly prepared me for the 1000 times things went wrong for me in 2017, that made me become who I am today.

Learning from mistakes and failures and adding it to your bank of experiences is the only way to unlock your full potential as a person in order to become a better version of You and lead a more fulfilling life. Education Begins at The End of Your Comfort Zone and After You Check Boxes in order live a life of no regrets.

All of these situations are all too common, yet never call for permanent change because everyone is stuck in the past and will brush it off by saying it will pass or get better later, "I don't care". It's hard to surrender to our past. I get it. Our internal ecosystem will be so used to hanging out with a group of friends or doing an afternoon brunch. Embrace making your own decision by telling them you are working on yourself. It will make you feel empowered and confident.

And when you start migrating your mindset from checking boxes to uncomfortably enjoying the journey, you will move forward with way less fear, a much better person, and checking off way more boxes than you could have ever dreamed that externally please those closest to you and allow you to become fearlessly uncomfortable. Don't get me wrong. Checking Boxes is mandatory, but it won't bring you freedom, fulfillment, or failure. Rather it restricts us from opportunities of purpose within human connection and automates the wasted time in between checked boxes.

On a daily basis, the average person spends hours a day on social media, yet what are they really getting out of it? The ability to not be bored and make time go faster. As soon as we get into a fragmented moment where we don't have anything to do, we immediately check Facebook, Twitter, Snapchat, and Instagram, where we are exposed to a wide variety of useless content. We have failed to limit our content for the good. Your brain is walking onto a battleground every time you are on your phone or computer. And the best thing you can do is limit the amount of battles you're forced to fight every day while depriving your mental capacity. That's why I started putting my phone on airplane mode so I don't "lose" to my phone the second I wake up.

When having a conversation with anyone, the first question out of their mouth will likely be, "How are you doing?" And I guarantee that 99% of the time the answer is "Good," because who wouldn't say they are doing good? Because they will immediately feel like they are letting themselves and other people down if they don't say something positive.

One of the most toxic questions that almost always gets asked is, "So what are you doing these days?" Which really means where are you working and what is your job title so I can figure out how much money you're making. Why not ask "How many people have you truly connected with this month?" Or, "How have you grown since the last time we spoke?" Or, "How have you found fulfillment through making the world a better place?" We spend way too much time on useless questions that don't really get us anywhere.

Because at the end of the day, what do you get out of living in autopilot? The ability to tell someone that you work at a big bank?! Does that two second thrill give you freedom and fulfillment? Probably not.

The point here is that none of these examples add any value to your freedom and fulfillment, rather they reduce the already extremely minimal time you are lucky enough to have. So, next time you get involved with one of these pointless conversations, all I ask is to think really hard about if it's truly worth your precious time.

The root of this may be from our biggest strength in America which is the opportunistic open-mindedness of our society that is always willing to give someone or something a chance. When talking with people from Italy and France, it was evident they didn't have as many avenues to meet others and spark friendships. The negative side of the opportunistic mind is that it causes inauthenticity because we are trying to impress someone or ask them for a favor later, which allows numbness of communication and misleading directions after the first encounter. The best way I have approached this is to be very upfront in what you may demand of the relationship and set boundaries so that you don't mislead someone or make them feel bad. Pushing the point off only causes problems for both parties.

The opportunities of meaningful conversations with technology are at our fingertips. I have found that meaningful conversations enhance my enjoyment of the journey each day rather than the times when I participated in externally satisfying numbing conversations. Be fair to yourself and others by using meaningful conversations to awaken your numbness and instead enhance the enjoyment of your own journey and everyone around you.

How Can We Have More Meaningful Conversations?

This all comes down to the point of having open communication within yourself and having open communication with each other about critical issues. We continue to divide our nation and break up relationships because we can't be honest with one another. We need to stop lying to ourselves, stop lying to each other, and start making progress on problems that are suffering, struggling and strangling the freedom from our nation.

As I traveled to 36 states in the month of February, there was one common trend in every city: **lack of belief in one's prior failures being able to help others.** It makes sense. In our society today, we glorify our best moments on social media and can't stop gratifying ourselves with our accomplishments of checking the next box. But the reality is that we can learn so much more from failures and there is so much untapped fulfillment from failure.

Being vulnerable about our past and sharing our failures are essential in order to prevent more suffering and division. Because we hide our mistakes to ourselves, countless other people who are suffering in our past shoes will not be properly educated and will make the same mistakes we made that could have been avoided. If you know something or have an experience, PLEASE SHARE with anyone so that they can get it to the person who is suffering that needs it the most. This allows three things:

1. Someone to be saved from suffering
2. Someone to be saved from feeling unworthy
3. Personal feeling of fulfillment and worthiness

It's like a gratifying paycheck of giving to help someone else with no consequences. And you sharing your story will not only save that one person from suffering but also plant a seed for the knowledge to be passed down generation after generation!

Four Mindset Fixes:

1. Someone Needs To Hear What You are Saying!!
2. Holding On To Your Gifts and Messages is Going To Starve The World of Freedom and Fulfillment
3. Your Experience is Priceless and Valuable, Don't Let It Go To Waste
4. You Can Be A Role Model For Anyone If You: EDUCATE your experiences and put them in a lens that allows the person to put themselves in your shoes. Let them know that they need to make a decision for their needs rather than your needs.

How Should We Define Meaningful vs. Meaningless?

Meaningful-> Two Thumbs Up!!

1. Making Someone Feel Loved and Worthy
2. Improvement Without Expense of Someone's Worthiness
3. Enjoyment Without Expense of Someone's Worthiness
4. Positive Reinforcement

Meaningless-> Two Thumbs Down

1. Gossiping about People and Trying to Instantly Gratify Yourself
2. Making Fun of Someone Else Causing Them To Feel Bad About Themselves
3. Judging People and Sharing That With Others
4. Negativity, Envy, Self-Doubt

How can we unnumb people who don't understand and aren't motivated?

This seems to be a common situation in the workplace, where free people continue to encourage and motivate numb employees to care more, work harder, be happier, be less complacent. But numb employees won't understand or acknowledge and stay complacent and comfortable. In this case, it is essential to find ways to create purpose for them through work or non-work activities and imperative you don't let them influence you in a negative way. Create comeback analogies to something they like or are passionate about, offer them love/support, and continue to bring out the best of them. Everyone is here for a reason and you can have such a special impact on that person if you bring it out of them! If that doesn't work, no sweat. You are amazing for just going out of your way in the first place to help. Admire and reward yourself that you tried, make a fun game out of it, but never get discouraged! Your time is valuable and negativity doesn't deserve to be a part of it.

For me, finding ways to listen and learn about someone's past experience has allowed me to find a way to connect their value with an opportunity to educate other people and justify a specific purpose for them being where they currently are today. Our internal mind is good at justifying the opposite and looking at the downsides, but we are here for a reason and everyone is where they currently are needed the most at this moment. Whether its a construction worker who built the I-80 highway I am going cross-country on, the waitress who prevents someone from having a deathly allergic reaction, or someone who is serving coffee to someone at a 7/11, each one of these situations are enabling others to positively impact and move forward our society in the right direction. We are all farmers, planting seeds that we may never see grow, but by being ourselves and creating purpose for one another to the best of our ability without harming others, we all are worthy of being where we currently are.

How Do We Plant Seeds Properly Using Communication?

- If you want to have a meaningful conversation with someone, start out right by having an attitude of gratitude. Have an appreciation that the other person is choosing to take time out of their day because they want to spend it with you.

- The best conversations are the ones where each person feels like they were heard and understood. By the time the conversation has ended they will feel more deeply connected to the other person and they will go about their day feeling encouraged and inspired.

- Getting to this place with another person is simple, but a lot of the time, laziness or ego gets in the way. When you enter a conversation you need to rid yourself of all distractions, including wandering thoughts of what you could be doing with your time instead. The time is not all about you and don't expect to get any more out of the conversation than you are willing to put into it.

- Instead, it should be a time where you listen to understand and learn something either about the person you are talking with or the intricate details surrounding a subject of mutual interest. When you are talking, the best way to receive a detailed response is to ask open ended questions such as, "How did this make you feel?" or "Can you describe why you feel that way? Good questions will always require the listener to stop and think for a moment to provide a thoughtful response.

- A good conversationalist will be a gracious host by remembering to keep their mouth shut and their mind open. They will have good manners and will not talk over the other person. Someone who is a good listener will do their best to pay attention to the details being discussed and not be thinking about what they will be saying next. They will not be competing for attention and make the conversation all about them by equating their experience to theirs. All too often we fall into the trap of telling someone how we shared a similar situation. However, as much as we think this is helpful, it is not because all experiences are individual and can never be the same. Always show the person in the conversation that you care by allowing yourself to get in and stay with the flow. Go ahead and tell your great stories and when it's your turn, remember to keep listening. However, if your mind does happen to wander off, let it go, and jump right back in at the appropriate time. It's always awkward when you try and catch up with ill –timed questions or responses.

- In the end, great conversations will be simply about two people who chose to genuinely connect with each other to listen and be amazed at what the other has to share. They are never about self- promotion and they will not choose to waste precious time talking about things that do not add value for the other person such as name dropping, dates, and other trivial facts.

C
H
A
P
T
E
R
3
..

CRAVING COMFORT MAKES US WEAK

How do we shoot ourselves in the foot and starve ourselves of freedom to stay in our comfort zone :(

My freedom was buzzing as I hopped in a white checkered cab after slamming some pitchers of club soda and water while hydrating others on the eve of my graduation from college. The cab driver dropped me off before giving her life story about overcoming a sexual assault at a young age, PTSD, doctors trying to prescribe her pills, and cancer. I gave her motivation and positivity about her journey and how she was going to do amazing things.

"Doctors prescribe pills like they are candy," she said. "It has really fucked up my sister."

Doctors giving out scripts to Xanax and Adderall continue to zombify our society every day, creating short-term solutions and long-term damage. According to the Washington Post, 50,000 opioid doses are taken daily per every million residents in the US, which is 2 to 6 times higher than other countries around the world. By over-prescribing medication we create an approach that allows a craving for an immediate fix. This craving haunts us every day by making us weak, torturing our control and inspiring us to indulge in fake happiness. Fake happiness falls under the category of a sugary ice cold Sprite, a qb sneak of Xanax, a nice joint to burn, or maybe a smooth crispy Stella and use of the deserve card "I had a tough day" that justifies anything you can imagine. This mindset will only set you further from your journey. All of these fake happiness items, I endorse you having in moderation and when you are in your intentional enjoyment state, but using any of them as ways to fix a problem is going to tear you apart.

In Metrics, the statistics are quite concerning, but my fear is that the numbers for mental illness is way higher than documented. While NIH states that 1/5 of adults will experience a mental illness in a given year and Time's research states that there has been a 66% increase in anti-depressent usage over the past year, the statistic that really matters is the amount of people that wake up each day fearful of being their authentic selves, feeling insecure and worthless, and hating their current situation justifying it by poisoning themselves with toxic noise and substances. This statistic is higher than it's ever been before because we live in a world where we are very good at lying to ourselves and hiding from the problems we need to attack. The good news is that You can wake up whenever you are ready and shatter this disease ☺

The Competitive Mindset Blinds Us

When I was traveling into South Africa, we had a tour guide who had survived the apartheid and provided our group with infinite wisdom that I will never forget. When he grew up, they would catch him talking to someone and would lock him up for the day. They would cut his hands and now he has a wire in one of his fingers. Most of his friends were shot and killed during the years of 1979-1982. This man was practically screaming in the car, wondering why Americans judge, undermine each other, cut throats, all just to be #1, when #1 isn't even possible to obtain. The pressure of being #1 results in tragedies like Chester Bennington and causes 20% of our population to have depression. What he recommends through his experiences is to do the best you can and find contentment through love and happiness and find the good in people and make them feel worthy rather than judging the bad.

The competitive nature of college and achieving highly lucrative real-world jobs promotes a vicious atmosphere where people will do anything to get the job or move up the ladder. Although on the surface it might seem like they are your friends, you have to be careful because some will act as if they want you to succeed but talk behind your back or look down on you because they can't accept the fact that someone else is better than them. When people don't respond, judge, get rejected, it creates our mind to immediately think we did something wrong when it was completely out of our control. We lose confidence in ourselves and think we are doing something wrong. This justifies the quick hit mindset and sparks a trigger for our inner mind to act up on us. Therefore, we decide to engage in cheap thrills that makes the entire cycle more lethal as it only delays our problems, makes us feel less worthy, and drifts the state of being physically and mentally healthy further away. YOU have the power to work harder than anyone else being yourself. That's all you need. The only way to beat the doubters is by putting your head down and taking action. Don't let your innerworld shoot yourself in the foot by stripping your own purpose and harming others by getting caught up in the expectation culture that's NOT YOU.

"For me I have dreams to build an online course on waking up people to be mentally and physically healthy every day" my editor informed me. Both of us laughed. A year ago, each of us would be freaking out worried about what the other person was doing and how to compete with each other. Instead, we both did everything in our power to help the other reach the most amount of people to positively impact the world. For me, creating my own inner laws and mantras to live by have freed myself to be able to coexist with anybody or thing in the outside world. And this has fulfilled myself by indirectly touching people around the world through giving a voice to others and helping them reach their full potential. In short, If I inspire Bernie to believe in himself and force him to make a post that inspires someone else to get where they want to be, I Win, Bernie Wins, and that person wins. Sounds like an easy concept, but this competitive society completely blinded me into thinking I win when someone else loses. That mindset promotes envy.

Our society thrives on envy. There is always another destination that seems brighter and greener at the present moment. In our society, the pressure for us to be at another destination in the present moment makes us feel like a dog on a leash. Everything we consume creates an internal expectation that we need to be as happy and good looking as people look on Instagram at all times. Whether it's social media, money, or a job title, we are always wondering why we aren't in someone else's shoes at this exact moment.

One of my podcast guests and brand strategist Chloe Belangia brilliantly used the fakeness of filters on instagram to transform herself into becoming the best possible version of her authentic self. She became uncomfortable by deleting the app for a couple of months and came back with a new mindset utilizing the platform as a way to impress herself and inspire her followers on the journey through being her natural self. Chloe is one of the many that have taught me there is always a way to creatively grow and turn a negative situation into a positive one when you go inside yourself, reflect, and take action.

Whether or not we realize it, all of us are searching for freedom and fulfillment and what matters is the journey, not where you started. It is your own decisions, not your uncontrollable circumstances that matter in this present moment moving forward. Someone with student loans may envy someone whose parents paid their tuition. I will tell you there's many people that have been lucky enough to have college paid for them and they are unfulfilled without motivation and haven't been given the opportunity to fail and grow! I will also tell you that having student debt can be a blessing in disguise as it will allow you to have skin in the game and fail quicker before finding yourself and your meaning in this world. Either scenario should be cheered on by the other party to work hard, be a good person, and succeed.

I recently met up with a 14 year old at the Startup Grind Festival in San Francisco. She knew how to code four languages, had been public speaking since she was 4, and is currently taking college level courses in 9th grade obsessively coding on the weekends. Two booths down I met up with two 18 year olds who were building wearable technology that will be able to communicate with restaurants about food allergies and alert parents about food allergy reactions. I couldn't stop smiling and offered to help her with anything she needed. I am a huge believer that we are just starting to unleash the unlimited potential of our brilliant minds to unchartered levels and positively change the world to become a better place. Each one of you is a shining star in your own way and no matter where you are today you can indirectly have a positive snow ball effect on the world and assist those who are shaping the world to move forward in the right direction.

Starting today, you have a clean state to stop the envy and hate and see everyone around you as an inspiration. Envy and failing down is the most sure-fire way to starve the world of freedom and fulfillment. All those people you could be cheering on and that could be supporters for you on your journey are just filling your valuable time and energy with negative vibes. Worse comes to worse, use that negative energy to implement strengths on your enemy and us that to motivate yourself to put your head down and take action! If you are yourself being free and start working hard with the proper foundations and beliefs, you will love every day and will have the last laugh because you will be richer in freedom which is the most important thing. It doesn't matter what job you have or what other people are doing. Rather, what internal growth metrics you create, your mental and physical state, and how you can be yourself without harming others each day.

Instead of complaining about why I didn't get the job at Deloitte, I befriended the star student who got the position over me, only to find out that he was a super listener who had created a community called Real Talk that was inspiring and changing lives every week through creating a community of sharing on our college campus. He truly made a me a better person through attending these sessions, teaching me how to listen, understanding my web of life, and providing alternative avenues of fun that didn't revolve around going out with friends. Now he has been cheering me on as I go into the battlefield of writing this book, while I will be cheering him on to fail freely to share Real Talk around the world. Rejections are blessings of freedom and have the potential to create life-long friendships.

How To Shift Envy To Fulfillment?

We all have flaws, we have all have made mistakes, and we all have gifts. But keeping those to yourself is going to be a disservice to yourself and others.

By vulnerably sharing everything I have learned up until this point with those younger than me and absorbing every piece of advice I am lucky enough to receive from those older than me, my life has changed my life for the better.

Your mindset, not your age, will determine how fulfilled you are on your journey. Each one of our journey's is unique but everyone who has touched me is on my journey, and I am apart of everyone's journey who I have touched. That's the beauty of life, we are all on each other's journeys and the only thing in our control is to spread education, love, and appreciation for each other's journey. Let's choose to move forward together as one journey and eliminate envy!

People Laughing At Your Dreams Restricts Us From Failing

We always immediately, and often unintentionally, stop progress thinking we are doing someone a favor. Why are you writing this book? Why are you not going out with us? Why are you having a conversation with him/her? These questions touch upon the risk environment we are brought up in. When someone does something out of the ordinary, we immediately question and make them feel like they are doing something wrong. We are so paralyzed by this fear to feel like we are doing our own path that we can't even get close to failure. We doubt, judge, and make jokes about how that person is never going to reach his/her dreams. This strangles people from achieving something they truly believe is going to the make the world a better place because it doesn't conform to the norms of society. The mindset you need is how can I inspire people to go down the path that makes them the freest. Why not motivate and inspire them to reach their dreams? Why not provide resources and challenging questions to help them move closer to their dreams?

One may challenge me with a question what if I/You inspire someone to drop out of college, take on debt, quit their job and they become homeless. I would respond by saying the right time is when you have created good habits in every aspect of your life that you can consistently follow. The right time is when you wake up in the morning and you are so miserable you can't enjoy the journey. The right time is when you wake up and you can't be yourself every day. In these circumstances, you can only Fail Up because regardless of whether you are living on a couch with credit card debt, living in a car in Santa Monica, or living under a tree in South Africa you will have the ability to be free and be yourself.

The people making fun of the dreamers are the ones who have a leash down such a narrow path. And when these people don't succeed, they can't deal with rejection because they have never failed at something before. This narrow, safe path is more dangerous than we think. The reality of the situation is that failure makes us grow from rejection. The narrow path we are told to follow doesn't teach us how to react to rejection, it only gives us the opportunity to strangle ourselves and others from being ourselves if we aren't careful. This traps those who can't fail because they see the few risk takers who fail freely and want to follow their footsteps, but they don't believe in themselves and become unsatisfied with the path they are on. Every path is unique and different and rejections are only going to create more learning opportunities and experiences to help you grow.

There is a big difference between failure and not being successful. Failure is treated as disappointment rather than a growth tool. The lack of failure is actually stagnating our growth. There are so many ways to fail on your narrow path that will not harm anyone else and positively impact yourself. I live by the quote "If people aren't laughing at your dreams, your dreams aren't big enough." And if people are laughing at your dreams, which has happened to me over 100 times just like failure and rejection, it just adds to my motivation!

When Someone is On a Mission to Accomplish Their Dreams

1. Listen for a second and understand where that person is coming from. They have some reasoning from their inner self on why they are considering this and challenge them to discuss if the would be able to handle the worst case scenario.
2. Then, ask if they need any help with connections, feedback, or anything else regarding the subject

3. Finish something along the lines of I am so excited for you trying this, if worse comes to worse make sure your embrace failure and learn from it.
4. Ask 1-2 challenging questions that make them think about what they are trying to escape from their previous role. Direct them to internally understand if this change is going to truly make them enjoy the journey more internally.

Now that you have opened your mind up to these unfortunate consequences you may have uncontrollably engaged in, you have:

1. Freed yourself from the pressure of doing better than other people
2. Freed your friend to go after his/her dreams and inspiring them
3. Freed yourself from unfulfillment because you are in this journey together with everyone in your circle.

Last Action: Immediately delete any account, any conversation, any topic, any person that makes you feel like shit!!! That may mean news sources and the President!!

PART 2:
The Mindset Movement To Awaken

CHAPTER 4

STRIKING OUT WITH PLEASURE

"How do we attempt to fix this within our mind frame?"

We fix it by shifting impulsiveness to discipline through authentic action. We fix by asking the question how can I earn freedom rather than asking why can't I have this. Every time we complain about what we don't have, we are effectively taking away fulfillment and freedom from ourselves. Every step we take towards earning something is another step toward being a freer more fulfilled and failing.

You are not going to fix a situation by taking shortcuts, doing drugs, pushing off your problems. Fixing something means going within yourself, embracing the suck, taking on a challenge, and enjoying the process of getting better. The issue that I faced before departing on this journey was that I used short-term hits on social media, alcohol, sugar, etc. as a crutch to forget about the problems that I had within myself. And I trained my mind to justify not fixing these problems through pushing it off. I was afraid to be uncomfortable and as soon as I had some free time, I would immediately go to my crutches to forget about my problems, rather than sit uncomfortable fixing my problems. By allowing myself to wake up with bad habits, I would create so much unnecessary stress on myself and other people for no reason.

I guess looking back, my way of being a kid was achieving a state that I never felt before. I was striving to be a kid with no worries, and instead I became all the undesirable, annoying qualities of a kid by not being in any control. Looking forward, I realized that the only way to feel like a kid was by growing and learning every day through meaningful experiences that I could be me. Not only do you feel like a kid when you engage in these activities, but you also are in full control and are fully awake. Anyone can feel like a kid and enjoy the present moment!

The first step is recognizing that pleasure is available at any moment while happiness is something that is earned. Happiness is something that makes you uncomfortable in the short-term to earn or attempt to achieve results. Pleasure is something that we don't earn and always there for us. In terms of happiness, the biggest misconception is achieving the results we discussed earlier. Happiness doesn't need to constitute success, it just need to accomplish learning and growing through Failing Up. In terms of pleasure, the biggest misconception is that you can't enjoy it. Pleasure is a key ingredient to enjoyment, motivation, and visualization when done in moderation. The issue with pleasure is that it

THE JOURNEY TO FAILING FREELY

lends itself to Failing Down because just like numbness, it is always there for you as an easy way to engage. Intentional pleasure and short-term uncomfort will allow you to thrive and be able to enjoy the best of both worlds.

Rather than numbing myself at 2am at the Hawaiian Airport and automate my trip back to NY, I decided to build my mantras and goals for the month of July. As I asked a construction worker where the open lounge was in the middle of the evening, we engaged in an hour conversation about her transformation from pleasure to happiness. She created her own happiness through detaching from dopamine feeding pleasure and shifted her focus to meaningful endeavors, delayed gratification, self-care and conscious choice. This has allowed her to create new freedoms within the required training that has allowed her to feel freer than ever before, a new level of freedom way above the freedom to experience instant gratification dopamine hits. She even challenged herself to commiting to one of most respected and celebrated long-distance races for women in the world, which consisted of 41 miles of outrigger canoe paddling in the open ocean of Hawaii. This statement below convinced me to run the Virginia Beach Rock and Roll Half-Marathon.

"I would never have been able to experience the freedom of being on the open ocean outside reef looking back at the Ko'olau mountains, jumping into the ocean from the escort boat, swimming in the swells and climbing into an Hawaiian outrigger canoe to paddle into one of the most beautiful Bays on Oahu if I hadn't practiced discipline and replaced bad habits with good ones. I was smoking and drinking before I signed up for paddling. (which created shame and an identity conflict because I could not meet my potential with those habits and I identify with my self-confidence through athleticism, but they had become a form of stress-relief). Now I'm relieving my stress moving a boat over the beautiful surface of the sea and riding waves preparing to cross one of the most dangerous channels in the world. It results in a sense of being alive and FREE, in command of my life and able to accomplish anything I put my mind to. No sense trying to "give up" bad habits. Best to just replace them with good ones."

After earning my first true of thrill of completing the Half-Marathon in under two hours a month after my conversation from Sarah, it definitely started to wake me up about how much happier and more fulfilling working hard and achieving something was than getting blacked out on the weekends, having a steak dinner with wine, or engaging on other pleasure avenues that weren't necessary to constantly engage in. The ability to earn true thrills is a much better drug than pleasure. Finishing the Half-Marathon was such a thrill with music and hundreds cheering me on, I didn't hesitate to sign-up for the NYC Marathon. Three months of going out and drinking replaced by feeling alive, feeling mentally and physically at my peak, and finding my authentic self just by committing to a true thrill!

Here are some of the true thrills I have found on my journey to replace cheap thrills

- Hiking and camping overnight with friends to see a sunset or sunrise

- Going for a Swim with goggles with your phone laptop and life philosophy being safely guarded by a friend
- Having a meaningful flow moment/experience/conversation without needing to take a picture or be on your phone
- Salsa Dancing with someone you have never met before
- Playing scrabble, jenga, a jigsaw puzzle, or another board game with friends
- Play soccer and educate younger kids on how to spread love, be nice to people, and be happy
- Having a delicious chipotle bowl with a La Croix cherry lime seltzer after skipping corona night and crushing a workout
- Mentoring others that are younger than me
- Donating time and giving to others who are taking action and making a positive impact on the world
- Giving People Opportunities to have purpose

We are trained by our surroundings to embrace short-term comfort. But how will you grow? The trick to avoid these dopamine hits is to create challenges and games within each activity you do in order to make you more satisfied on a short-term basis in addition to enhancing your self-control. Finding ways to add value to others through your activity can even be more fulfilling. I started creating small games within each of my activities in order to get the most value out of the activity for myself, make the activity worthwhile for others, and find gratification in the moment that aligns with my long-term vision. I challenge everyone reading this book to embrace short-term uncomfortable situations and attack them with challenges that create "little wins," because I believe it will lead to more happiness in the long term while still giving you short-term satisfaction!! Training your mind through self-discipline can also improve your long-term vision while creating those short-term wins through delayed gratification.

I always thought that telling, bragging, and doing was super cool. Again, and again the chatter would be "I had an unreal weekend dude you missed out at bars" or "yoooo I have been doing abs for an hour this week! Get on my level." Part of this stems from the fact that I wanted gratification for doing what I was doing. Showing people you are working hard gives you instant gratification, not sustainable gratification. It also tricks your mind into thinking that you are more productive then you actually are.

The only way to create sustainable gratification is when no one knows. Because that is when you know you are doing it for you and no one else. That is what makes me dig deeper into a workout when I know it's just me. By making missions to have the most fun by satisfying myself and not being able to share, you can gratify yourself for the right reasons through what I call **invisible gratification.**

Invisible Gratification is doing something that is really fulfilling and stealthily not letting anyone know about it so that you can truly say you did it for yourself. One time, I was chugging a gallon of water at an end of the year party with a hundred people or so and after talking to some people, the best idea I came up with to enjoy the present moment was to hand out waters to everyone at the party. In a span of 30 minutes, I went to Food Lion bought cases of water and with the help of random people helped distribute over 100 waters without asking for anything. As soon as everyone was hydrated, I immediately left without telling anyone and felt ecstatic. The other time was in St. Thomas when I was waiting for someone to come out of the bathroom I ran into a custodian who was cleaning the bathrooms and wanted to instill her with positivity. She talked about her family devastated by the hurricane and as a small Christmas gift, I gave her an $100 gift card to buy something for her kids that specifically related to positivity. We then exchanged pictures of our family and moved on with our day. It's these types of moments where you feel like you are on top, because no one else knows. Invisible Gratification and True Thrills will lead to sustainable happiness, but it's a lot easier said than done to shift your mindset from short-term pleasure.

The Unintentional Harm Caused By Short-Term Pleasure

Short-term Pleasure is what strangled my freedom to embrace the opportunities at my fingertips. When I was at IBM and William and Mary, they gave me the most amazing opportunities in the world that I will be forever grateful for. But I didn't wake up until my final semester at school. I was so asleep I didn't even realize the potential I currently have because of the short-term pleasures constantly flowing in front of me that I couldn't resist. I would immediately go for Corona Night with the boys, play golf, go to beach or do any activity to make sure I maximized being comfortable around the same fun people all the time so I didn't sit around doing nothing. And there is nothing wrong with that!! I truly enjoyed each of those moments with my buddies.

However, the constant stream pleasure activities led to an ignorant mindset of what was holding me back. I was having the best time every day with my buddies participating in activities that it blinded me from seeing the potential I had if I didn't go out all the time and wake up hungover. I would immediately make sure I had my phone and wallet, say "It's a great day to be alive! Get a gallon of water, hop in the sauna, rip the diner with some of my buddies, and then head to the beach or golf to get it all out of my system and move on like everything was ok.

The issue was that short-term pleasure was falsely enslaving my mind to forget about the prime issue in the first place. I was blindly failing by not being physically and mentally healthy and not changing my habits. The problem here is that if something crazy didn't happen to me, I wouldn't have been able to see what was holding me back from being the best possible version of myself. I would define this as Failing Down: Not learning or growing from a mistake because I had checked off all the boxes and could justify anything in my mind. Short-term pleasure is the root of Failing Down, which further numbs you into believing you are free. Every single time you embark on the enslaved going out journey it will egg you on to get closer and closer to a state that you have never felt before which could end your life. Wake up and get out of this trap, it's only going to get worse the longer you delay. Luckily my ignorance was shattered by my trip around the world over the summer.

It all started drinking copious amounts of alcohol in Mykonos out of a 50-foot straw dancing on the beach having the time of my life ripping ski shots with people all over the world. But I woke up the next morning not feeling physically and mentally healthy and decided not to drink for the day. That evening, I was at a pleasure high driving two girls around in an ATV looking over a beautiful sunset in Mykonos. But as we arrived at the beach party, we ran into a man who wouldn't stop bothering these girls about having a shot with him. They continued to refuse which somehow prompted the man to bring up 9/11 attacks so we immediately protected the girls and decided to go back to the beach party at our hostel.

"HEEEEEELPPPP" two girls screamed behind a white garage alleyway. They were missing a phone and neither were in control of themselves due to the alcohol they had consumed that evening. But the issue was that their ATV had broken down. As tears flowed down their eyes, we calmly got the ATV up and running and were able to find their hotel to return them safely after nearly causing a huge car crash. Externally, my life seemed like the moment at the sunset, internally the freedom of my out of control life was as helpless as those girls. That could have been me in 8 years. I would be coming home from a New York City club after spending $300 because I could, impressing others, feeling entitled, and screaming helplessly for a cab. Improvement and growth would be replaced by auto-pilot and saying yes to going out every Friday and Saturday night, each dinner on the weekdays with the same buddies, and recovering on Sunday unproductively only to pass time to do the same unfulfilling activities on the weekend. It wouldn't be my fault either, it would be the thrill of short-term pleasures!

14 days later, South Africa would permanently change my journey to Failing Up. After inspiring one of the most awesome people I have ever met to climb up Lionshead mountain for the sunrise, I thought my luck had changed after Ethiopian Airlines lost my luggage for 7 days in the Indian Ocean. But on this cold misty day at Table Mountain, I took the most dangerous path down the mountain only to find that the yellow footsteps that led me to the cloud of air also led me up to basecamp at the same exact time a soccer player from Tanzania was running up. He spoke softly, but with great wisdom. Pleasure, Fear, Entitlement, Materialism, Pleasing Other People, Love, and Not Harming Others were some of the issues discussed. In that three-hour flow conversation, my life changed forever. This is a man that ran up and down Table Mountain 6 hours a day to train for his soccer dream, get poorly treated by out of control drunk people at the nightclub he worked at, only to go back home under a tree between two logs and do it all over again. This is a man that was completely free and happy, and had absolutely nothing, and I was drinking away every drop of fulfillment I had the freedom to be born with.

I stopped drinking for 60 days and it completely changed my life. Besides the absurd amount of time I freed up, the opportunities of earning achievements, meeting new people, and feeling like a Million Bucks are just three of the endless growth and opportunities that arose when I was mentally and physically healthy every day. I embraced it whether it was making a new podcast, writing a book, or making allergy safe healthy pancakes. This was the most key ingredient not only in relation to my self-control and discipline but also really appreciating every moment. For the first time, I actually created downtime for myself. I know it's not as glorious as taking a snapchat having fun with your crew shouting "Free Money" but you win because you are treating yourself with "True Freedom."

I don't regret anything, I just want to share this information to give you the freedom to know that short-term pleasures could be blinding you from figuring out what is holding you back to reach your full potential. It has only made my journey more fulfilling as I continue to become the best version of myself. It isn't as easy as shotgunning a beer and isn't going to be fulfilling as eating a cupcake sitting on your coach in the present moment, but patience and persistence will get you so far people won't even recognize your growth. Failing Up leads to happiness, pleasure leads to Failing Down. You make the choice when you are ready. If you Fail Up, you can do anything in the world.

My last thought on the matter would be that until you are ready to grow up, find a state with instant pleasures and people that you truly enjoy being you, can remember, and not harm anyone else. There is nothing wrong with being comfortable, but make sure you enjoy those purposeless moments to the fullest and don't complain that you don't have fulfillment in your life.

Our past creates our story, good memories, and enjoyment of the journey. Your story allows you to learn from the past to become a better version of you in the present moment. Being a better version of you in the present moment with your past education allows you to freely chase your dreams moving forward. Comfort restricts chasing your dreams moving forward.

Action: Choose an Instant Pleasure and Stop Doing It For 30 Days

If you stop doing a short-term pleasure for 30 days you will be able to get uncomfortable while saving so much time and money!! It will be so worth it ☺

CHAPTER 5

RENATUS

"What's Available When We Wake Up? Why Should We?"

We should wake up because everyone alive in this world today deserves to be themselves, and currently that is not the case. Our friends, parents, and ourselves would do anything to make us happy, yet our actions continue to drift further and further from that. Rather, the act of being comfortable and dependent allows us to hit the snooze button from this reality we all are striving for which starves happiness and freedom from too many. After my wake up to Failing up, I was "Reborn" and the future couldn't have been brighter, the opportunities were endless.

The Thrill of Being Independent

Once you shift your mindset to being dependent on yourself with True Thrills, the Renaissance has begun and you are now a step closer to effectively shifting your mindset.

At the end of the day, the only person who is going to be there for you when you need it most is you. There is no running away from you either.

1. **You need to be dependent on yourself to prepare for an unfortunate situation out of your control**

    Failing and being uncomfortable are the keys to being prepared for any situation. You need to be strong for other people and yourself in the occasion that something bad happens to someone close. You need to know what it feels like to suffer, feel pain, get rejected, and have obstacles so that you can become stronger and lift those around you when life throws a curveball around you.

2. **You need to be dependent on yourself to be physically and mentally happy**

    You need to implement good habits, discipline, and self-control in order to be physically and mentally happy each day. Whether that's going to the gym every morning at 7am, meal-prepping healthy food for the week, not having that beer and wings with the boys, it is up to you if you really want to feel good every day. You create the ecosystem of content that flows through to your brain, you create the people that you want communication with in your circle on a daily basis.

3. **You need to be dependent on yourself to improve and grow everyday**

    There is a big difference between going to school or having a job and being successful, happy, free, fulfilled, being a good person. Going to school or having a job provides an amazing platform for you to build for yourself, opportunities to create relationships with people to provide purpose and inspire you along this amazing journey you are about to embark, and allows you the freedom to spend money on material items, traveling, or courses to learn. But a company or school is focusing on changing the world for the better making profits to entice shareholders.

    Therefore, there needs to be an understanding from the workers side that they may not be doing the most interesting, fulfilling work or doing work at all. If that is the case, you need to take advantage of the people and resources the organization has and continue to work on relationships, continue to learn skills to propel you to get on the next amazing project. You need to grow yourself personally as much as the company grows you. Sitting there waiting for a job or school to give you some purpose filled role, paying a lot of money, with your own freedom and hours is not going to happen my friend. You have to work using your own metrics to grow yourself because at the end of the day they didn't hire you so they can fill your dreams. They hired you to have an opportunity to make an impact within the firm. You need to go within yourself and figure out how you can extract the most value out of everything they have to offer.

4. **You need to be dependent on satisfying yourself to enjoy being yourself**

    There is a big difference between surrounding yourself with the right people to lift you up than relying on a group of people to do things. This creates a dependence on people to enjoy yourself. Eliminating this dependency was a key to my transformation through bringing the right people into my web.

What's Waiting For You On The Other Side? A New, Confident You With People Cheering You On!

Once you are independent, you will be able to embark on path that only you will enjoy and thrive. You are special. You will not compare yourself to others because you are on your own planet. You will not question the past or think about why the present isn't perfect. You will not question why you didn't know something before and dwell on the past or have too much excitement for the future. The grass is only greener in the present moment being yourself enjoying it with the people who make you happy. You will have the freedom to live in the present moment. The freedom to feel a rain drop. The freedom to enjoy any situation that you are currently alive. Be confident you have everything it takes. Embrace the knowledge you have gained up to this point and go capture your freedom.

There will be no more "I wish I knew this or that when I was 20" That's fake, unfulfilling news. Riddle me this: How would you earn freedom? How would you fail? How would you be fulfilled? How would you find meaning? You wouldn't. It would be too easy and boring.

The Ability to Cherish Each Moment With the Ones You Want to Be Around

Before I woke up from auto-pilot, I was aimlessly running around to please everyone, and even worse not spending enough time with my loved ones. This summer, I would not let that be the case. When I came home from my trip around the world, I realized how little time I had left with the people who inspire me most, and I made it my number 1 priority to bike with them every day, play chess, walk the dog. By making my parents feel loved and appreciated we were able to form a deeper bond like never before. It goes to show that people, especially your family and friends, are 1000x more important than your iPhone, which I guarantee you spend more time on then with your mom or dad. Let's change this for the better. Most of us are lucky enough to have the ability to hear, talk, and have a mom or dad. Why waste the valuable time spent with them on a useless device or thinking about the next destination? When doing a hike in Espinido Falls in Malibu with the family, I eliminated all distractions to forgot everything in the moment besides enjoy the beautiful day, nature, and spending quality time with my family. Every time a thought would occur in my head about what are we doing after this, I would quickly shut it down to myself and continue on. I know this may sound stupid, but doing this for every activity especially without distractions from your phone or trying to plan something else can provide those special moments and provide that gratification when you have such a good time at the activity that you shared with those closest to you.

The Ability to Avoid Negative Talk, Gossiping, Judging, and Not Spreading Love!

- The first advantage of waking up is avoiding negative talk (gossiping about people, starting a pointless argument, making someone feel bad about themselves). If it isn't about helping people, lifting others up, reaching goals, or spreading positive vibes, refrain from negativity! Gossip is not only a waste of your time, but also creates unnecessary short-term gratification instead of long term growth.

- The second positive change was shifting to giving love to everybody, no matter what the circumstances were. We have no excuse for not communicating with each other. People are lonelier and more disconnected than they have ever been in a world where technology is easier than ever before. We are letting each other down by letting technology drive us apart and automate our lives rather than using it to make others feel loved. In such a sensitive world we live in today, it is MANDATORY to take every opportunity we get to compliment someone whether it's someone you know, someone you don't know, or someone you haven't spoken to in a while. You never know what difference it may make in their day, week, month, or life. It is all of our responsibility to look out for each other. And I guarantee by doing this, you will not only make that person feel much better about themselves, but you will feel happy and fulfilled. Emanuel from South Africa taught me that responsibility is to love no matter what, regardless of how another person acts or treats people. And there is nothing holding us back following through with this beautiful responsibility except yourself. Regardless of why we are here, how we go here, what our purpose is or where are path currently has taken us, it is imperative we treat everyone with love and kindness. That is the least we can do by having the privilege to be alive in this world

- A third fallacy would be judging people in your own mind and sharing that with other people. Have you ever heard of the 2*2=1 life lesson? A teacher writes 2* 2= 1 on the board with a correct set of complicated multiplication being right below. As soon as he turned around, multiple people call out immediately to say the answer for the first problem was wrong. The point is that people in the world will not compliment you for doing right, just judge you by the one thing you have done wrong. Shift the mindset to how can You show love for people doing the right thing and how can You help a person grow and inspire their journey for a mistake they made.

The Ability To Be a Functional Human Being

After heading down to the 530 Scenic Gorge route in Wyoming, the white crevices in the triangular shaped peaks stood proudly over the shining blue marina at Buckboard Pier. The peacefulness of the scenery externally was a bit different than the stuffy brown walls and an out of order coca cola machine inside of the recreation shop.

"The kids these days are not educated, are rude, and disciplined. I am from a family of 19 children and I can't believe what kids get away with these days. I am so scared for my grandkids."

To be a functional human being in society, you can't harm people, you shouldn't spread hate to other people. I got caught up thinking that just because I worked hard on the weekdays, I was entitled to do whatever I wanted on the weekends and be a complete degenerate fool. ITS NOT COOL.

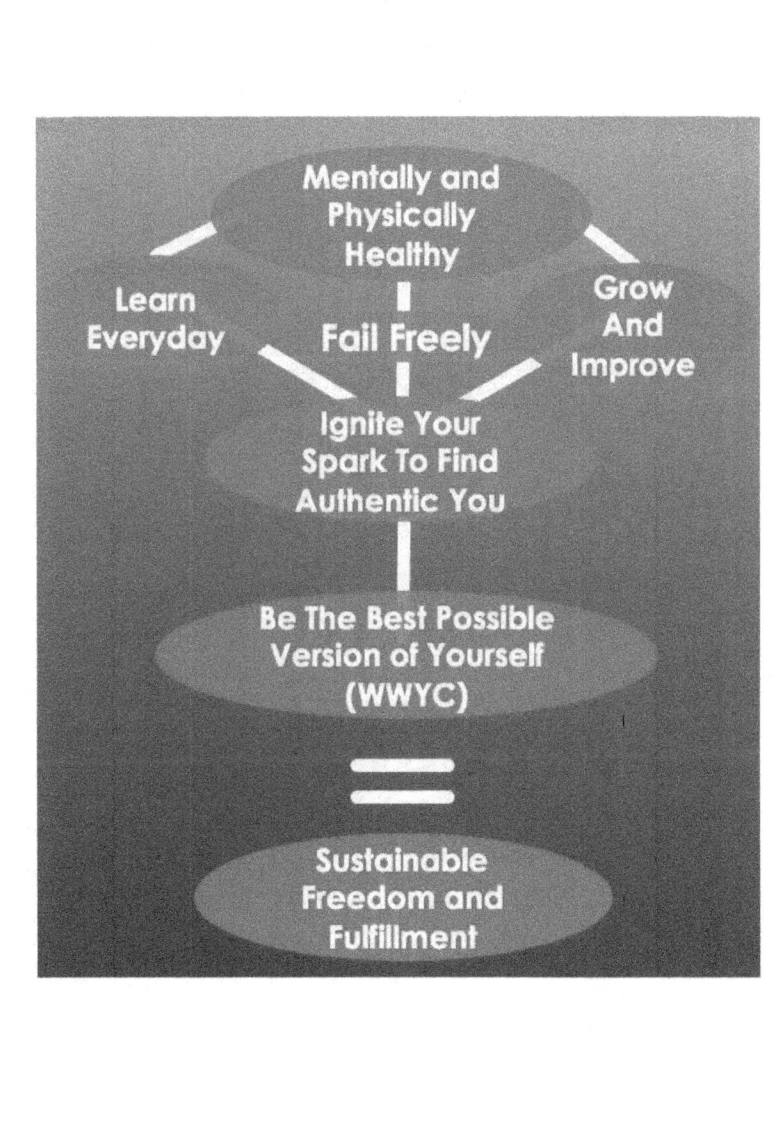

- Mentally and Physically Healthy
- Learn Everyday
- Fail Freely
- Grow And Improve
- Ignite Your Spark To Find Authentic You
- Be The Best Possible Version of Yourself (WWYC)

=

- Sustainable Freedom and Fulfillment

PART 3: Failing Up

CHAPTER 6

THE DREADED DETOX

"How Do We Eliminate the Most Difficult Toxins in Our Life?"

Old Me Used To Worry About These Questions On A Daily Basis Because I Wasn't Physically and Mentally Healthy :(

1. *In the future "I will be happy."*
2. *Why Can't Time Pass Faster?*
3. *What is Wrong With Me?*
4. *Why can't I be like him/her?*
5. *Why do I do this to myself?*

1. Unless you break out of this habit you will always feel like something is missing or unsatisfied in your entire life. Because you aren't invested in the present moment which means you are missing the beauty of life itself. The lottery won't even satisfy you because you are achieving to be happy not happily achieving.

2. The reality of the situation is that someone always has it worse than you. Someone is on death bed and about to die from cancer. Someone is fighting for their life oversees. Someone just lost a loved one. People would die to be in your shoes, to be able to have one more laugh, use their 5 senses to feel alive one more time.

3. You are making yourself feel sorry and unworthy. You are letting other people bring you down. You are doing a disservice to yourself. YOU are Worthy. You are Awesome! You have the power to help people change the world for the better. You need to stop thinking and worrying about other people. They don't care about you as much as themselves. YOU ARE SPECIAL!

4. Delete anything that makes you feel negative about yourself if you haven't from part 1. Root them on for reaching an achievement. Encourage them to keep enjoying the journey. Let this motivate you to improve and grow every day then treat yourself to a moment that will make you feel so good and fulfilled. When you are down or struggling think about the good moments you have had in the past or visualize what you are truly working for the vacation itself.

5. Stop Harming Yourself, Stop Harming Your Body, Let Go of a Toxic Relationship with a substance or people. You have the power to stop all this, but you haven't and you are doing a disservice to YOU. Let go of anything that harms you. YOU DESERVE TO LET GO.

To start being fair to yourself, you need to eliminate the questions above and ask how can I be, mentally and physically healthy every morning I wake up?

Once you embrace waking up, you now have the power to recognize what is holding you back. Now you can get rid of anything holding you back to be mentally and physically happy every day. Understanding what you can and can't control and how to approach each of those situations will be the last push to the finish line. At that moment, I wrote down everything that was bothering/stressing me at the present moment and split it up into two categories, controllable and uncontrollable. I became a detective for my own life and figured out how to attack this list. For the uncontrollable stuff i.e. my career, I used positivity and my filtered internet content to help me understand there was truly nothing in my power I could to change these stresses. So, I blacked out those stresses real quick. Erasing the controllable ones took the understanding that this was going to be a LONG process maybe 3 months, maybe 12 months, but that would be part of the journey and I treated it like a fun game. It wasn't easy, but now I wake up and don't stress about anything. Worse comes to worse, I get a job at McDonalds start at the bottom and work my way up. Well actually, maybe not McDonalds because feeding people with unhealthy food doesn't align with my values. But you get my point. YOU ARE IMPORTANT AND WORTHY ENOUGH to free yourself from what is bothering you. Get away from anything that doesn't serve you that is in your control.

Let's take a complicated, unhealthy relationship I had the pleasure to help solve at one of the most beautiful beaches in St. Thomas. One where the man thinks he is happy because he takes his woman out to dinner, showers her with gifts, and everything seems great on the surface, but he fools around with other girls and doesn't do things that his lady wants to do. He has the powerful unintentional harm ego where he mentally thinks that he is doing everything right and the other stuff he does doesn't matter, when it is really negatively impacting the women and making her feel like a piece of meat. This analogy is plaguing so many people. Whether it's with relationships, bad habits, our smartphone, alcohol, drugs etc., This analogy is deadly as it is a backbone for Failing Down. Because a majority of the time that type of relationship will go on for years with the constant stressing, complaining and the ability not to feel mentally and physically free every day with no progress. This is because we are weak in the mind. We can't imagine a world for one day without being comfortable or having a crutch. When something has gotten bad enough, think of that situation with the kind, beautiful lady above. How would you address that situation? FAIL UP by immediately deleting IT from your life. It doesn't matter how much the exit costs, get out as soon as possible! If YOU don't stand up for yourself, you will continue to fail down and strangle your happiness.

You need to be selfish to yourself and feed yourself with the most quality ingredients on all fronts in order feel mentally and physically healthy each day. Don't let someone else drag you down. Recognize, reset, and create situations where you can only bring people up.

Thinking on Margin in the present rather than sunk cost is important to understand to be mentally and physically healthy every day. That's why we take student loans out to go to college so that we can learn this concept in Econ 101 and apply it to life. That means that whenever you have a problem you want to solve it as fast as possible. In the words of successful entrepreneur Michael Martocci, "You have to think on margin today by making the best decision for tomorrow no matter how much time, energy, or money is spent in the past." This refers to relationships, business, love and so on. Living your life waiting for something to work out you are trying to force isn't going to cut it. Waiting on the past to workout is deadly. Not only does it mean you are doing something you don't want to put time into, but it also stagnates your growth from new opportunities and new people. It must have been really hard for Mike to eat up $20,000 on a business venture he felt like he was forcing, but 8 months later he is 100x better cause of it loving the new company he has created. But if he didn't think on margin he would be contacting flaky developers in Taiwan trying to launch an app he was trying "to force." He would still be enslaved into something he couldn't control with his skills and his values didn't align with. Same goes for your health. Just because you spent the last 8 months not working out or eating healthy, you need to bite the bullet and start fresh today or you will always thinking about the past rather than being the best version of yourself today.

What Held Me Back in the Past?

The shift from career mentors to authentic personal mentors and friendships has completely changed my life because they educated me about the opportunities and hope of finding my authentic self through connecting me with likeminded people. By giving me the trust and responsibility to set me up with amazing people in my network, it forced me to not engage in any funny business. At the time, I didn't have any problems harming my body or making myself looking like a fool outside of school, but by having the opportunity to meet people who were changing the world for the better, it made me question what was I truly doing with my life. It made me want to find myself and spend time with myself so I could make a positive difference in the world. I still have career mentors as close friends and they have also made a positive impact on my life, but they didn't pop up in my head to hold me back from getting into funny business. They just made me more motivated to work harder focusing on my grades, which unintentionally made me go out more and engage in pleasure activities. Once I started finding myself, I then realized that power to positively influence those younger down the right path and how fulfilling it was. I highly recommend you find someone younger than you and offer advice. Not only does this allow you to have more fulfillment, learn more about yourself, and enjoy the times when you were in the same shoes, but also will make you to want to grow yourself with him/her. When I hit an accomplishment, it is my tribe cheering me on that gets the satisfaction. When my mentees hit an accomplishment, that's when I feel the most fulfilled. When it comes to finding mentors, continue to give, continue to build trust, and be honest and upfront to what you are looking for in the relationships. Patience in relationships only makes the journey for each part more fulfilling. Mentoring also forced me to realize the importance of making my actions speak louder than my words. I am not using the word forced as a negative stripping my freedom. I am using the word forced as a way to set internal boundaries in your habits to resist the urge from something that sounds good in the short term but drifts you away from yourself. Once I found purpose educating others, there was no way I would use cheap thrills to endanger my ability to create fulfillment for myself and others. I finally shifted my fear from pleasing others to look cool to fearing letting my new friends and mentors down that had spent their super valuable time on me. The new fear allowed me to get rid of everything that was toxic in my life and preventing me from becoming the best possible version of me. This "Detox" eliminated my final fear of letting my new friends down and shifted that fear to asking the question: **What Value Can I Give To Each Person I Am Lucky Enough to Meet To Make The World A Better Place?**

The shift from receiving to giving helped me get over my internal fear that has been haunting me ever since I started my journey. I always feared my external reputation and what others thought about me. Before my journey, I would take, take, take! Rather, you want to provide favors to others without asking for anything in return. I thought it was cool to live lavishly through having other friends take me to events, dinners, and activities. But I soon realized that this allowed them to unintentionally manipulate me. Because they constantly gave, I got sucked into the nature of receiving and in turn made me feel trapped. Not only would I feel obligated to hang out, but also felt the need to please them for no reason. This exponentially increased my unproductive, comfortable time and stagnated my growth. Through my travels of the summer, I switched completely to a give mindset. I would immediately find ways to add value to other people I was talking to in order to connect with someone who could benefit, give them a book, or write a nice message on a dollar bill to show my appreciation for them. By shifting to the giving side, I have felt 100x more fulfilled, but more importantly freer than ever. Some become givers to manipulate. I give to spread the positive love and free myself up from any obligations I may not want to engage in. Therefore, I don't need to do anything to please anyone else because I think I owe them something.

New Me refused to ask myself any of those questions mentioned in the beginning of the chapter as I got rid of everything bothering me in my control mainly toxic relationships and substances in my life. Crossing the finishline at the marathon was when I turned the corner from my past. Although I had my blue and grey BW crutches physically with me as a crossed the finish line, all of the crutches I had used to escape, numb, and drift further away from myself were gone. I still wasn't guaranteed to achieve my goals and dreams, but giving myself the best chance in my control allowed me to feel fully free to embrace whatever is meant to be. The foundation had been planted for finding myself, but I hadn't found my passion yet. And there was nothing wrong with that. Until you find what ignites your spark, I recommend you remain on the path that opens up the most opportunities for you in the present moment that allows you to be healthy. Don't worry! Be Patient and focus on growing and improving every day. Your spark is in sight.

Two Myths of Being Healthy

1. **Sacrifice Work For Your Short-Term Health** If you find your work-life balance getting out of control, it is time to start implementing daily exercise and good habits baby step by step. There is always time in the day no matter how many hours you work to get 15 minutes of exercise and 15 minutes of clearing the mind. I have been guilty of sacrificing my health and learned my lesson the hard way. But at least I am Failing Up now and you will be able to Fail Up from my experience! After 6 straight days of working over 12 hours, I hit a 52-week low in my own mental and physical health standards. I went to bed that evening and made a mandatory day off from work and my phone at a mini ski mountain up north. My only conversation of the day was with a man from Singapore on the chairlift, who happened to be spending his 1-month vacation in New York skiing at a beautiful resort with practically ice and one functioning black diamond. Regardless of the lack of powder and our age difference, we both ended the day on a 52-week high and couldn't have agreed more about the value of vacation and appreciating the present moment with exercise. Sacrificing your health

for anything will only demise your productivity, energy, and increase your negativity. I am still riding my 52-week high with that lesson in the back of my mind! Anything is possible when you are healthy.

2. **You Can Fix Your Health Easily Tomorrow** I always thought that as I grew older, whenever I wanted I could just flip a switch and immediately stop damaging my body, eat healthy 7 days a week, and start getting into good habits surrounding my health. This couldn't be further from the truth. This mindset is completely lethal and this is why so many have such a difficult transition from HS to College, and College to "The Real World." There will always be more than one distraction that pops up every day that will try to derail you from you healthy routines. At the beginning of my journey, my low self-control would easily cave in and I would enjoy the moment (Which was completely ok!). However, as you start feeling your 52-week high, as you start staying loyal to your foundation, as you start building self-control, it starts to become a privilege to say no, and you start to realize you want to get everything you need to get done early in the day to open up free time for those epic experiences you would love to say yes to but don't have the time. This came about 6 months into my journey and started to actually appreciate and fully enjoy the moments that I deserved. Before this, I honestly couldn't give the moments that were special the time and attention they deserved because I was thinking about the next thing or worried about what someone else was doing. Bite-size by Bite-size,

THE JOURNEY TO FAILING FREELY

I started increasing my self-control, increasing my daily routines, and now every moment I decide to say yes to will be an epic memory to remember.

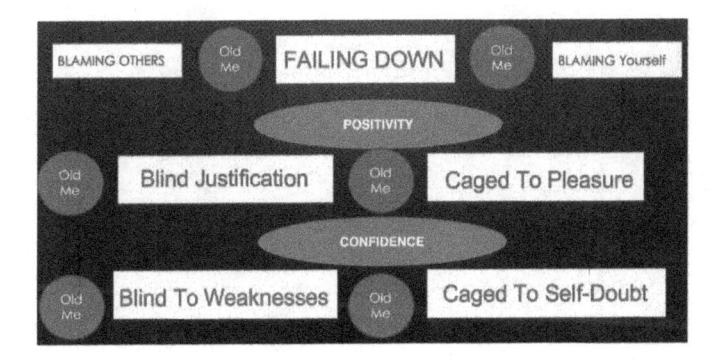

BLAMING OTHERS	Old Me	**FAILING DOWN**	Old Me	BLAMING Yourself
		POSITIVITY		
Old Me	Blind Justification	Old Me	Caged To Pleasure	
		CONFIDENCE		
Old Me	Blind To Weaknesses	Old Me	Caged To Self-Doubt	

CHAPTER 7

"BREAK FREE OF THE CHAINS"

"We Must Continually Break Free of Old Patterns and Replace Them With New Ones"

Once you are physically mentally healthy and are enjoying the process each day, you have the ability to improve and grow every day in the present moment through the 1,2 Principle. Using this, you will not only shatter your goals and achievements, but also will never think about old patterns because you will be constantly excited to find new ones each day at your mental and physical peak.

The 1,2 Principle is about continuously improving yourself in every aspect of your life through your journey to freedom for internal evaluation on how you live every day with the proper mindset and your growth! Whether it is family, business, relationships, health, spiritual, or self-awareness, there are always aspects of your life that you can improve to make yourself freer in the present from the time you wake up to the time you go to bed.

Qualities of being in state 1 means you are strangled and not freely in control to be yourself in addition to preventing others around you from being free every day. Qualities of being in state 2 include making the best use of your time while growing the freedom of yourself and others around you fully in control! Every evening I can go to bed knowing I maximized state 2 qualities while following my personal principles and mantras. Now you can substitute cheap thrill instant gratification for sustainable satisfying thrills to maximize your day while feeling high on life. The cheap pleasures that I experienced Failing Down were a necessary part of the journey, but recognizing the emptiness through the 1,2 principle was a game changer. Ask yourself what can you do today to learn and grow from the past, the people around you, and your present day actions? What can you do today to improve any bad habits/ anything bothering you by a baby step?

State1 Metrics for Stagnant Growth

Definition: Failure to Improve Asleep on Auto-Pilot

Consequence: Not Being in Control With a Fixed Mindset

State2 Metrics for Daily Growth and Improvements

Definition: Baby Growth Each Day Awake in Manual

Consequence: Being in Control with The Foot on the Gas Pedal

12 Symptoms

1. *Confidence*

    State 1: Improper Confidence: Cocky/Self Doubt/Self-Blame

    State 2: True Confidence "I can therefore I will" with Recognition of weaknesses

2. *Relationships*

    State 1: Toxic, Unhealthy Relationships Stunting Your Growth

    State 2: Surrounding Yourself with People Who Allow You to be Free

3. *The Role of Pleasure*

    State 1: Uses Pleasure to Try to Fix, Delay, Avoid Problems

    State 2: Uses Pleasure in Moderation with Friends for Intentional Enjoyment

4. *Positivity vs. Negativity*

    State 1: Asks Why Me to every problem by complaining instead of taking action

    State 2: Asks Why Not Me to every problem to embrace situations

5. *Being Who You Are vs. Who You Are Not*

    State 1: Tries to Please and Impress Other People

    State 2: Being Fair to Yourself

6. *The Way You Treat People*

    State 1: Treats people Condescending, Talks Bad About Others, Stops Dreams

    State 2: Make It Easier for People to Be Free -> Spreading Love, Greeting People With a Smile and Supporting Everyone On Your Journey

7. *Purposeful vs. Purposeless*

    State 1: Cut Throat Purposeless Mindset-> You Need to Be Better than peers

    State 2: Growth Mindset with Purpose-> You want everyone to succeed

8. *Comfort*

    State 1: Unintentional Comfort, Lack of Learning Mindset when Uncomfortable

    State 2: Intentionally Comfortable, Embraces Uncomfort w/ Failing Up Mindset

9. *Preparation*

    State 1: Lack of Preparation leads to not being able to fully enjoy Present Time

    State 2: Spends adequate time to effectively prepare and mitigate worries/fear

10. *Past vs. Present vs. Future*

    State 1: Lives in the Past or Future, Focused on Destination, Never Happy

    State 2: Lives in the Present Enjoying the Journey w/ 10% on Hope and Dreams

11. Communication

    State 1: Meaningless Conversations, Strangles Other Freedom by Wasting Time

    State 2: Use Conversations to Recognize and Attack Problems Plaguing Growth

12. Gratification

    State 1: Takes action to impress others through instant gratification/dopamine

    State 2: Takes Action to impress self through delayed & invisible gratification

You make the choice. There are two straws you can choose starting tomorrow. The first is to live like you are currently living now, wishing you could be happier and be like someone else, not being grateful, and wasting your time and gifts enslaved to other people and enslaving those who look up to you to stoop to your level. The second is to live like you are currently living now in your role, but relentlessly focus on how to improve yourself in your weakest areas, striving to spend time being yourself with people and activities you enjoy, creating purpose for yourself and likeminded people, and spreading love to everyone around you to make them feel worthy!

All of these qualities have to do with how we most effectively live every day based on whatever situation we are presently in. Using these metrics has allowed me to achieve mental and physical peak performance every day and will allow me to thrive whether I work an overnight shift at the Hawaii airport, work 18 hours a day as an investment banking analyst, or work 9-5 at a corporation, because

I know I can sustain happiness through fulfillment and freedom every day with the people in my life. When I was in Idaho, I spoke with the port authority worker who monitored 800 trucks for his 10 hour shift every day, making sure the trucks and their drivers were safe to the roads and the people around them. The bright young man goes home everyday knowing he saved multiple lives. Some are going to find fulfillment through their job. Others are going to find fulfillment through non-work activities and serving others. The only barrier preventing you from finding fulfillment is not giving yourself a chance to fail.

Everyone's growth should be evaluated on your own scale for each of these metrics. Risk tolerances and improvements are different for everyone and it is important to compare your growth to yourself and no one else.

The 1,2 Principle Mindset to Enjoy Yourself Along With Good Habits

Enjoyment was another struggle in the beginning of my journey, but I quickly created a game that infinitely allows me to win. If I truly want to enjoy an experience that may arise at any time/day with any person, I must 110% commit to the enjoyment and not worry about the consequences. The only rule I have in these situations, is that it needs to follow my criteria of enjoyment through my values being in control and it motivates me to work even harder the next day to constantly improve myself without harming anyone. I am constantly enjoying or improving, without stressing or worrying, because improvement leads to situations I am prepared to enjoy and enjoyment leads to giving me areas

I can motivate and improve myself. Just like life, just like fear, enjoyment is like a mindset. Embrace your decision without overthinking. For me I have done this through creating a boundary between bad habits and intentional enjoyment. Having a sprite after an epic bike ride with the family would be intentional enjoyment. Procrastinating for a test or staring at the clock for your job would fall under bad habits because you are essentially numbing and wasting your precious time.

Once you get to this stage, the one thing you need to focus on is believing in your beautiful self. It's important to stay humble and constantly ask what is it that I would like to improve, but the reality is that you aren't giving yourself enough credit. You have worked so hard to create an amazing foundation that has allowed you to make yourself and everyone around you better, yet you are shooting yourself in the foot by doubting and suffocating your achievements. You are good enough just the way you are!! Attack what's causing you to overthink and doubt, and you will minimize that negative energy to positive confidence!

LaBella's Four Forces to Maximize 1,2 Principle

1. Make Sure You are Fully Immersed in the Present Moment Being Who You Are, Not Who You are Not (It is easily to get influenced or get thrown off who you are by someone else)
2. Make Sure You Aren't Harming Others Intentionally or Unintentionally

3. Ask what do I want to get out of this moment with intention, this trip etc.
    a. Do I want/need Enjoyment
    b. How can I help someone else become a better version of who they want to be (ONLY if that person wants help, is willing to listen, and takes action, because if not you are wasting your valuable positive energy and creating more negative energy within the person you are trying to help that doesn't want it).
    c. Create a meaningful discussion or conversions that involves growth or flow state
    d. Always Ask: What am I missing? And Listen to the Answer
    e. Is there any fear I need to overcome/get rid of people who don't serve me?
4. When you are stuck, think about which one of these you can extract the most value from at the present moment. If you are at work and don't have anything to do, use this time to enhance a skill for your boss or on project you are working on. If have worked quite hard Monday-Saturday, treat yourself to an enjoyment evening. However, be careful never to depend on an event or people for enjoyment.

Just like I was chasing blindly in life, if you don't live each day with the intention of fulfilling ones of these improvement/growth metrics, you have effectively wasted a day of your precious time without moving forward.

Think about all the progress you have made since reading the book. Now on the way to your current state think about a time when you broke down, had a mental breakdown, or had something that tried to steer you back on your previous unfulfilling journey. For me, it caused me to step back and think about all the progress I have made and how something little like this is a peanut in comparison to what I have overcome, what I am accomplishing now and what I will create in the future to make the world a better place for others and myself. Either way, visualizing the past progress you have made can be super helpful to giving you the confidence and also allow you time to self-reflect and be aware of your past vs. present state when you bring the 1,2 principle into your life.

CHAPTER 8
..

BUILD A NEW TOOLBOX TO MAINTAIN GROWTH

"The Tools and Techniques You Will Need to Maintain Your Awareness/Freedom to Fail Up"

Present Moment Positivity

When having a conversation with a cancer survivor in St. Thomas, she mentioned to me how everyone was sick and miserable going around explaining how they responded when they heard the news. But not Santana. With a constant smile on her face, she stood up proudly and delivered a speech on Why Not Me and rallied the people in her group to change their life. I completely agree it is impossible to understand the pain in the situations that are unfortunate such as cancer, but I do know that positivity is a lifestyle that is contagious, can lift people up and can be life changing for communities that are suffering the most by helping you overcome challenges that are out of your control. I define positivity as making the best of the current situation with optimism to improve the experience with the people involved. The previous day in Puerto Rico, sprint boxes and debris filled up the decimated streets that still didn't have power even though the hurricane happened months ago. Meanwhile on the cruise, we had just participated in a 5k walk to raise awareness and money for breast cancer and some guy is yelling at a worker who wouldn't serve him breakfast because it was past the cut-off.

Negativity is a surefire way to kill freedom. There is only one way to respond to a devastating hurricane out of your control. How can you justify thinking negative or dwelling? Each precious moment we have on this beautiful Earth with beautiful people is about enjoying the hand we have been dealt. How can you enjoy by complaining, arguing, and negatively impacting the situation and other people around you? YOU ARE WASTING TIME. The people affected in Puerto Rico and St. Thomas use positivity as a key ingredient to be more happier and fulfilled than most of us. The alternative to bringing negativity energy to a situation is becoming a robot. Going on your phone and thinking some sort of miraculous post or news source is going to cure your pain. It's only going to lead you to cheap, unfulfilling thrills like booze, drugs, and gambling. The reality of life is that the situation we were born into was completely out of our control and happened for a reason.

Each struggle that has impacted my life I have used positivity to overcome. At birth, I was diagnosed with food allergies, to egg, dairy, all nuts, and all fish. It would be easy to complain, moan, and yell at the people behind the counter if they don't have any dairy free options, but this has challenged me to say Why Not ME. If it wasn't me, someone else would have suffered and would have brought negativity to the situation, making others feel bad about themselves and causing unnecessary energy to every situation that involved eating. Instead, I have become a voice for the afflicted, raising over $1,000 for Food Allergies, writing articles to bring the food allergies community together, inspiring others through a new community called Allergy Travels, and adding as much value as a I can through positivity to those who need it most and have it the worst. If only there was an epi-pen for negativity !!

Another experience that was so eye opening was when I was in the training stages of the marathon and had run double digit miles the afternoon before dinner with my parents at a familiar restaurant in Williamsburg. I face-timed my mom as soon as they dropped me off looking like a full-on tomato from head to toe. As my mom freaked out, I laughed, popped some Benadryl and went to yack in the bathroom. Upon the medicine kicking in, I opened The Promise of a Pencil by Adam Braun and started getting in a flow state reading his amazing book which I highly recommend about traveling the world and building a for purpose charity that provides education to the 250 million people in the world who can't read. Even though I was so physically suffocated and not feeling myself, I could still have the privilege to not only see but also read a book and there was nothing that was going to stop me from crossing that finish line. The marathon injury definitely showed me the same thing. It made me slow down, appreciate each moment, and most importantly inspire hundreds of runners at the NYC Marathon to finish strong and run through the pain. It made me grateful for the ability to walk and have two legs.

Anything is possible if you are alive in the present moment no matter what hand you are dealt. There is no path too steep to overcome. If you can sit in the present moment and think, you are qualified to achieve your dreams at any age. There is a reason for you to be living on this Earth alive. Next time you face a challenge that arises out of your control? Ask why not me, and be thankful you have been called to grow, improve and inspire.

Confidence with Two Scoops of Visualization

Confidence is the next step in the puzzle to allow you to be able to prepare for anything. Once you acquire confidence as a skill, you will then be able to be uncomfortable and constantly grow yourself through other people in state 2. Confidence can be deadly on both sides of the spectrum. I know few who are able to maintain such a balance. The majority case I see that upsets me is people who don't believe in themselves. They fail to give themselves enough credit and make themselves feel like they aren't good enough. The even more potent case of confidence is overconfidence or cockiness. This is devastating for someone who has it all together, because they will never be greater than average because they are not willing to identify their own weaknesses and potential area of improvements. Additionally, this gives the person a miniscule chance to be fulfilled. We are never going to have our destination figured out, but we can open up our mind and ask what I am missing or what could be improved in my life to live in the present happier and more prepared. That's the point of the journey we are on. To be constantly improving all aspects of our lives. I would consider myself very high up in performance, and yet I still have 50-100 things I want to improve each week!! Confidence is the unwavering belief that you will achieve the goals you set out for yourself with time and patience. Along the way, it is crucial to recognize your weaknesses and where you can grow to live every day happier. Self-awareness for things you aren't good at is essential.

There is no thought other than you are improving yourself and growing every day to get there. There doesn't mean the summit. There means that you are going to continue to satisfy yourself and others around you through the next building block of growth on your journey. Going into the marathon, I knew if I got through the first couple of miles I was going to cross the finish line as the new World Record holder through the combination of this confidence and visualization. I zoned everything out besides feeding off of the thousands of people cheering me on, constantly making the finish line seem closer than it was in my head, and training my mind and body to go to unmatched heights while enjoying each click of the crutch on the soggy Poland spring cups on the black concrete. Visualization has given me the mindset "I can, Therefore I will." Mile 22 was the final straw where I would never look back. I couldn't feel my hands, my right knee was numb, and one of my crutches bottom piece had fallen on the ground. I had used all the tools above to keep the world record pace and was about to be done. But that image of me at the finish line would take over and wouldn't let me quit. I flipped the crutch on its backside. I wasn't going to quit now. My intention was simple, break the world record. The rest was history. Your mind, the people you surround yourself with, and your intentions are going to carry you the rest of the way.

Where Does the PCV Smoothie Leave You: Equipped to Fail Up

Curiosity and Persistence are the final two ingredients that will evolve through the 1,2 Principle and your new toolbox that will propel you to Fail Up. As you continue to move forward on your journey, you will embrace and appreciate learning every day and never stop trying to be a better version of yourself in all aspects of your life you can control. This new toolbox will prepare for the most unfortunate events that are out of your control. It is easy to blame yourself or someone for these types of events, but the reality is that the best way to deal with these situations is by being present in moment through your feelings and emotions. Why numb yourself out through a pleasure crutch when dealing with the struggle being yourself will only make the journey more fulfilling. The key is to minimize the amount of time dwelling, complaining, spreading negatively, because at the end of the day, we can embrace any situation with positivity which will allow us to learn from situation and grow. Not only do you harm yourself through a negative outburst, but you have given people an action to gossip about and talk negatively rather than talk about something positive or growth minded. Once you overcome this initial phase, it is time to Fail Up. Every set back is an opportunity to Fail Up. I have probably encountered 1000 problems over the last year. And each problem I have used the FACTS mindset to be free in the present moment! You will realize an unfortunate situation in the present moment is a peanut compared to what you have had to overcome on this journey, what you are accomplishing now and what you will create in the future to make the world a better place for others and yourself. Whether you believe it or not, there are ways and reasons to justify in your mind so you don't dwell on the What If. For me I call this Failing Up, which revolves around saying how can I positively make the most of the present moment if it were my last and make that moment even more impactful on enjoyment or growth than the expected one.

- **F**ind a Way Reduce Amount of Time Spent Acknowledging Annoyance of Situation
- **A**sk Why Not Me? A Problem Creates Greater Freedom and Fulfillment in the Present
- **C**onfidently Understand You are Equipped to Deal with any situation
- **T**hank Yourself for Being Present, Smile, Laugh, Embrace and forget about anything you can't control
- **S**tep back and think about all the progress you have made

Short-Term Failures that Positivity Turned Into Sure-Fire Successes through Failing Up

Situation #1 On a 24-hour layover in Hawaii I had finally arrived down where I was expected to drop my bag off to a Hawaiian Airlines representative for my flight to NY so that I could backpack around Honolulu around the day. I quickly got heated with the baggage employee who said she wouldn't be able to accept my bag until tomorrow. I started yelling at her in the moment negatively impacting 10 people in that short time span. 12 hours later when a security guard told me that I was not allowed into my airline gate for two hours and had to walk to the other end of the airport until then, I greeted him with a smile, wished him a great day and he pointed me at a construction worker to direct me to the proper gate. Turns out, after hiking beautiful Diamondhead mountain in a volcanic cone, enjoying a delicious banana pineapple smoothie with good friends I met and surfing at the famous Waikiki Beach, the greatest lessons were from a construction worker at the Hawaiian Airport @ 2am that I asked for directions to the open part of the airport. She went out of her way to walk me to the terminal where we had a conversation about the meaning of life and her perspective on the world. Here @ 2am in a Hawaii airport, the least expected time and place, I was given valuable advice about her journey and was inspired by her take on her job. While maybe she doesn't work at the most ideal time and place in most people's eyes, Sarah loves working at the airport because she knows she is making a difference all over the world, allowing travelers to experience a vacation, meet loved ones, or come home to less traffic, better roads, and time saved for people traveling.

Situation #2 I was in Costa Rica to celebrate my birthday and was looking forward to seeing an epic sunset. But traffic got stopped for an hour in the middle of nowhere and making it to the sunset was completely out of my control. I started laughing looking around as many angry people had their hands up complaining to one another. I looked to my left and a man with battered champion Philadelphia basketball jersey with a machete sweating profusely building a garage. Even though he didn't understand English, I hammered nails, sawed some wood, and successfully helped build a property in Costa Rica. Then as I got stopped in traffic again, it was directly by a school of kids playing soccer. I immediately hopped in the game and had an amazing time playing with these 8 year olds. I ended up giving one of them my favorite jerseys after he scored a goal on me. Bucket List Facts !!

Situation #3 As I planned to do final edits in Guadeloupe, I wanted to be prepared as ever before I embarked on a trip of a lifetime. There was going to be no more what if I was more prepared in 2018. I had my monthly goals meeting to start the day off and looked outside to find SNOWWWW. I was so excited that I wanted to accomplish my first task of the day by exchanging money at the bank by running to it in the frigid conditions. I did that only to find out that the local bank didn't have Euros on them. No worries, there was a bank in Greenwich that had them, and I had already gotten my workout in for the day so it was a success. Upon going to the bank, I didn't have my ID, which was in my gym bag at home. I quickly realized there was no shortcut or way around it, except to accept the fact that I was going to have to go home and wish them a nice day to make sure my positive presence was felt. As I walked out, I saw an old lady who was shivering and miserable.

I asked her if she needed a ride home. Upon saying yes, she told me she was from Germany and was waiting for a cab for the past 2 hours. I told her I wish her well and she was going to have the best year of her life in 2018. She shook her head and laughed, "It's not going to be a good year, I have leukemia, I don't have a lot of money. I am going to home and take a Xanax."

"That's no good, I am writing a book on how to stop people from doing opioids. What would be your advice to someone my age in general to avoid taking Xanax and drugs?"

"I lost my second child, a daughter, to suicide. She had schizophrenia. She was a star student cum laude and never harmed a soul." My advice would be: Don't do anything you are going to be sorry for the rest of your life. You don't want to be enslaved to alcohol, pills, and drugs because you will lose total freedom and control of yourself." Being in Control of yourself and improving and growing every day to become the best possible version of yourself.

Situation #4 When hiking through the beautiful Bogota Columbia, I ended up getting lost through the trail, only to find a crew horseback riding ahead of me. I followed them, thinking that they were going to the top of the mountain. Turns out, they were going on a 6-hour horseback ride across Bogota. There was no turning back. I had to keep up with the horses for 20km with a speedy pace with my white Nike shoes in 2 inches of fresh mud. I am so grateful for these people accepting me as part of their group of providing me with apples and water to get through the run and inspiring me on the journey. Getting to the end was one of the most fulfilling feelings.

Situation #5 After seeing an epic sunset in Costa Rica with a friend from Costa Rica, my rental car broke down at a gas station causing an hour and a half wait even though both of us were starving. We taught each other Spanish and English over the next hour with Lewis' Howes Mask of Masculinity book, danced salsa to the neighboring music, and created an Instagram for Sandra's "best day ever".

Preparation is at the Root of Failing Up

Once you attack every situation with the PCV smoothie, you now have the entire tool box to prepare for anything. The negativity free PCV Smoothie has one last touch that will lead you to freedom and fulfillment: Preparation.

00:36 the Air France kiosk read after I walked out of the women's bathroom back to my fort in the corner behind the dark shadow of Kafe Kreyol at the Guadeloupe Airport. In front of me lay 1/5 of a liter of volvic Eau Minerale Naturelle Water, 1/6 of Nescafe coffee in a Lafort Eau Bottle lying next to a dairy-free wrinkled Canadian bread bag filled with a ham sandwich wrapped in toilet paper. My iPhone cord connecting my old beats headphones with the new headphone jack awakened my ears through Spotify's offline download "You are Beautiful" by James Blunt as a man walked by sweeping the floor rejecting the only 5 euro bill I had left from the trip. I couldn't be happier at this moment. I had 6 hours until my flight and was prepared as ever before to finish the last touches of my book. It was the

PCV Smoothie that I carried with me as my friend hugged me goodbye at Terminal 2 at Guadeloupe Airport. It was my intentional uncomfort that made the moment more special. When you are prepared mentally and physically for the present moment, you will be ready for anything to be perfectly content alive and free in the moment wherever you are. That is how I would define vacation. The last time I was at the airport at this hour my life was changed for the better through Sarah. It doesn't matter if you are at an airport at 1am or on the 3rd nicest beach in the world, preparation allows your mindset to believe "This is Where I Need to Be in This Moment."

Let's take Sammi who is getting off a cruise for St. Thomas for the day. She rushes out of the cruise focusing solely on her destination and forgets her journal, book, and sunscreen. This shouldn't matter because she is meeting her friends at Emerald beach and needs to get there by a certain time. But unfortunately, she is thinking about that moment she sees her friends and ends up going to the wrong island, only to find out when she gets to the correct beach her friends had an emergency and weren't there. This results in a sad and miserable Sammi shedding tears. This situation is completely out of Sammi's control and recognition with preparation would have been a perfect recipe to refocus and maximize the experience on the beautiful day. Nothing out of your control will be able to harm you in the long term if you are prepared. You should always have everything you can possibly think of that would allow you to enjoy the present moment. The most epic experiences come from people, uncomfortable situations, and preparation. Don't sell your soul to an expectation or destination, create preparation that guarantees your own enjoyment and growth for any moment.

Preparation Tip

Always Give Yourself 2 Minutes of Stretching Before You Go To a Location, Destination, Activity, and truly think about what you need and would regret not bringing. When it comes down to preparation, you can't move forward without it. Preparation is what allows me to maintain my good habits wherever I go to. Preparation is the key to unlocking fear. Preparation is the key to making opportunities count at the most unexpected times.

Final Check Before You Can Fail Freely: Do You Have The False Positivity Confidence Ego Mindset?

After hinting at this concept in the pleasure discussion, the 1,2 principle and teaching you the right type of positivity and confidence necessary to move on, it is time to put your new mindset to the test.

I am 100% for using optimism as a way to get over the unfortunate, uncontrollable situations that arise in our days and the unfortunate mistakes that we have learned from, but the power of optimism has the ability to lead to a false sense of ease that you are moving in the right direction and growing. This ease can lead to poor preparation and decision-making that can drift you further away from your own definition of success. For me, to make sure I am remaining on the right path I ask these 5 questions to test myself each week?

1. Am I having enough conversations in my relationships that expose my worst case scenarios and allow me to get authentic, honest responses regarding my weaknesses and concerns of my career and life goals?
2. Am I blindly justifying pushing off any fears until later that are within my control?
3. Do I constantly blame myself or other people for things out of my control? This means you are caged to self-doubt and need stop using positivity to quell short-term fears of not being yourself.
4. Am I dependent on pleasures that harm my health during my enjoyment time?
5. Am I responding to situations Failing Down, or Failing Up? This question comes down to identifying the initial root of the situational problem. Identifying/Recognizing you are failing down with positivity is a good thing. Now it's time to Fail Up with action to prevent it to happening again.

CHAPTER 9

HOW TO FAIL FREELY

"Why we must feel free to fail in order to find our authentic self?"

Currently, You are being yourself, growing and improving every day, physically and mentally healthy floating around State 2 Either:

- Comfortable, content and free being yourself not strangling your own and others freedom, knowing the grass is greener for you wherever you are, not spreading negative energy harming other people.
- Experiencing a spectrum of highs and lows maximizing each day with no regrets around the right people stressed about what you are working on won't have the impact on the people you would like to help most. You are vulnerable, fearless, and continue to inspire freedom all around.

Either scenario, we are in this life together and you can fail freely as long as neither situation is enslaving others or yourself, harming others or yourself. You also have the ability to get a good sleep each evening, wake up and eat a delicious healthy breakfast, get 30 minutes of exercise or meditation in, put your phone on airplane mode, and journal about what will make this upcoming day "A Great Day to Be Alive."

Once you get to this point you have the freedom to take whatever path you want. If you want to get plastered all the time and live that life, I please advise you to do it with the least harm to others around you. I will also advise that you will unintentionally harm more people than you think. And the fulfillment achieving authenticity through being yourself is quite higher than any cheap thrills, job title, or money you may make. But this book is not for me to tell you what to do. It's to give you the freedom to know that we can't control anyone or anything besides ourselves, but we do have the freedom to educate people to expose them to the failures and opportunities we have have experienced that will lead them down the path that will most likely satisfy themselves.

I could've taken the easy route out and stayed an extra night at the Airbnb for 40 euros, but what was that going to do for me besides put me in automatic mode to NY. With the preparation mentioned above, I was up for any challenge to create an uncomfortable situation into an epic experience at the airport. As I chilled comfortably in a stretched position not being disturbed eating my ham sandwich safely guided by the toilet paper, two guys arose stumbling toward me. I couldn't help but wish two guys a friendly "Bonjour" with a thumbs up.

"We have just been kicked off a plane from St. Martin to Paris that made a stop in Guadeloupe to call the police because we were drinking a bottle we bought in the duty-free store on the plane" one said with a half-empty bottle of Red Guarana Desperado. The other man was facetiming his girlfriend disappointed he had delayed his time to see her while filling me in that he didn't have any money to get back to Paris. The men had prepared a little too much for harming their mental and physical state I guess, but they hadn't prepared their mind for unintentionally harming others as well as preparing their mind to embrace the worst-case scenario.

"Why are you doing this to yourself, does drinking make you feel free so you can miss your flight and let your girlfriend suffer? You can learn from this and turn your life around!" as both men intently listened still amused over the fact I thought they were younger than their actual ages of 32.

This situation would be the opposite of my win from the Greece situation. Rather this would be a classic short-term pleasure Fail Down, when you will wake up at random airport with Desperados at 32 without freedom and fulfillment, failing to learn from the last hundred of mistakes you have made in regard to short-term pleasures.

A failure like this provides an opportunity to learn and earn true thrills or take the easy route and keep unfreeing yourself from cheap thrills. If you currently are failing blindly and have the lethal mindset I used to have, that is ok and fixable over time!! That means you are good at failing which gives you a head start. If you currently have yourself figured out and all the tools I walked you through above, you probably have treated yourself so well that you are rookie at failure. That is ok and fixable over time as well! You have been given the tools to fail freely and have the freedom to know not to get blinded by the Lethal Failing Down mindset when something really bad happens that is out of your control.

The Four Footsteps of Failure

1st Step -> Based on everything you learned throughout this book, determine your current fear parameters with these four questions in order to eliminate all the fear out of your control

1. What was the biggest obstacle that held you back in 2017 and why did you fear attacking it? What would you have done differently to put off that fear?
2. What are your biggest fears in 2018?
3. What is the worst-case scenario of those fears Emotionally, Financially, Mentally, Physically, Time Based ?
4. Who/What is stopping you from overcoming these fears today rather than pushing them off until 2019?!

Result: Once you do this, then you can flip a switch with your mind to assure yourself that you did everything in your power and there is nothing you can do besides embrace the situation and migrate from fear to enjoyment.

2nd **Step->** Once you have created your fear foundation, it's now time to identify categories of different types of achievable challenges to get out of your comfort zone that will guarantee growth within:

- Strengthening Relationships
- Meeting New People
- Confidence
- Traveling
- Online Learning Communities
- Fulfillment/Volunteering/Charity
- Health and Fitness
- Self-Awareness
- Physical Competitions (Running, Biking, Swimming, Marathons, Triathlon's)
- Mental Discipline

3rd **Step** -> Eliminate Time and Money Spent on Non-Improvement/Enjoyment Activities and Pull The Trigger Putting Your Own Skin in the Game

If you don't have any money to put in the game, that's ok! Time is more precious than money and counts as skin in the game. And when you do implement these habits and continue to grow, you will start by reevaluating whether you want to spend your money material things, lavish meals, pleasing other people, or bettering yourself. The first is easy, comfortable, and unnecessary. It will enslave your mind and provides no growth, besides creating a higher standard for your enjoyment levels, a craving to do the same thing over again more often, and make you more likely to fear missing out and being uncomfortable. It may be a good idea to truly evaluate your personal needs, wants and desires. With all the skills you have learned on your journey, you deserve the chance to fail freely. It's is much more fulfilling than material desires. For me I shifted time away from pleasing other people, going out on the weekends, and doing things to pass time through.

10 Skin In The Game Purchases I Made w/ IBM Savings and Going Out Time Savings

1. 2 Week Entrepreneurship Course in Israel-> Learning and Meeting New People
2. School of Greatness Academy -> Investing in myself and other people who want to be great through 10-week online course to build foundation and good habits
3. Stopped Drinking for 60 days. Invested my weekend in meeting new people, becoming vulnerable, talking to people sober to help inspire confidence instead of being comfortable stagnating my growth at a bar harming my body.
4. Half Marathon-> Pushing my Asthma, challenging my body to its limit, and inspiring others
5. Full Marathon-> World Class Motivation, Visualization, Discipline, Delayed Gratification through 2 months of running 40-50 miles a week
6. Fundraising $3,400 for Pencils of Promise-> Learned How to Ask and Receive, Something that made me

quite uneasy but ended up being one of the most fulfilling experiences

7. Yogi-> Pulling the trigger on creating a C Corp to create a positive social media platform investing time, money, and my risk appetite
8. Creating Podcast-> Started my own podcast to share qualities of high-performing millennials confidence, positivity, inspiration
9. Created Positivity School Facebook Community-> Produced weekly inspirational positive messages to group of over 100 people
10. Traveled to 20 countries alone

Action -> Where is your time least effectively spent or negatively impacting your life?

Pick 3 categories that you would like to improve on 2018 and set an achievable challenge to achieve by December 31, 2018 within your fear parameters intentionally uncomfortable!

4th Step: Embrace Failure to Find Your Mental Beach

If you are in control being yourself, mentally and physically happy, and improving and growing every day, you also need your daily dose of vacation or intentional enjoyment. Intention of vacation in life through your own enjoyment and freedom is how you cross the finish line.

I want YOU to find the spark that I have found through meeting people and traveling. I want YOU To create space for whatever it is that wakes you up every morning!!

When you intentionally go into personal challenges uncomfortable, you are setting yourself up to wisely fail. You are hedging your risk so greatly that you can only grow and succeed. Once you commit to being intentionally uncomfortable, you will immediately feel 100x more invested in yourself and the activity. Once you put skin in the game for failure, there is no half-effort. It is full-throttle intentional attack mode. You need to seize every opportunity earning thrills, creating epic experiences, and building your own community of people that constantly hold you accountable and inspire you to do extraordinary things and not let limits define you.

This is going to create people egging you on in the battlefield of failing freely because they put their own skin in the game to improve and grow and are in your same shoes. Skin in the game creates trust on both ends. Trust eliminates fear because you have someone embarking on this amazing journey with you. While there are a multitude of activities you can do with what you have been given, the more skin you put in the game, the more people you will be willing to grow and improve. The more people will flock into your circle trying to inspire you. The more people you will inspire to be free and do amazing things. Freedom and Fulfillment come at the root of being uncomfortable, but they make you more in control. Your community is responsible for pushing you to mental and physical limits you couldn't imagine that are in your fear parameters. To clarify, being intentionally uncomfortable means that you are putting something at risk that you **personally value**. Whether that's a certain percentage of your capital or a risking a vacation to Mexico, it doesn't matter. The only thing that matters is that you care about it and would be devastated without it. Intentional uncomfort with the proper toolbox and people guarantees a positive ROI on life. You will always be growing, improving, enjoying the struggle, increase motivation and takeaway some lesson that will propel you to be keep moving forward.

These people I have met via failing freely have additionally solved the fulfillment portion always missing in my life. As each of us currently stand at any time in our life, we continue to build our journey through our past based on the people we have crossed paths with, our experiences, and the material we have been taught through education. The most epic fulfilling experiences have come from the people I have experienced the failure journey with and the amount of freedom I have created for myself and them as I continue to move forward. As you continue to fail and learn, you will not only exponentially increase your growth, but you will be able to skyrocket the proper amount of self-confidence, turn rejection into motivation, approach every situation in life with positivity, and eliminate any fears about nonsensical thoughts or worries about what other people will think. You have worked so hard in the past to be prepared for this moment when you put skin in the game. Make it count. Reinvent yourself every day and constantly learn in the present to make yourself and others better in the future.

I live on vacation every day. Obviously school, work, sleeping, eating take up a good amount of time, but the rest of the time I am in complete vacation mode doing something I love, not worried about anything, being intentionally uncomfortable, and being around people that make me free and happy. It is important to define what you want vacation to be for you rather than how can you impress other people. For me, I struggle being comfortable and sitting around doing nothing or watching TV. I don't consider that vacation. I probably wouldn't consider driving a manual stick in a foreign country the best situation either. Vacation is truly how many moments in the day can you really create your mind to believe that "I am completely free, happy, present, and satisfied right now."

Up until starting to travel, I excelled at shooting myself in the foot by stressing, not being mentally and physically healthy, and doing things to please others during my vacation time. Traveling alone is how I found myself and figured out what I wanted from life. Through all the time I didn't have data and was traveling alone, I was strangled to spend time with myself, and it forced me to understand who I wanted to be and how I wanted to feel every morning when I woke up. I figured out that I thrived being uncomfortable and didn't like being comfortable. My reasoning came from asking myself this question, "Is this contributing to me getting better on this great day to be alive?!" And I realized that engaging in comfortable pleasures didn't do it for me. The uncomfortable actions made me fail wisely and learn. When you fail, when you put skin the game for something you value, the only option is getting better each day with unbounded freedom. Freedom erased my fears and created euphoria for myself each day.

Entrepreneur Artem Mashkov has created several successful businesses but his "most positive ROI was when he missed a $92,000 opportunity with a clothing brand," because he never made that mistake again and used what

THE JOURNEY TO FAILING FREELY

he learned to be in more successful for himself. At the end of the day, giving yourself the opportunity to fail doesn't necessarily mean you will fail. That's the real value of the education over the last 17 years of schools: to give us the ability to excel and shatter goals with the possibility of failure on the line. The pressure of potentially failing will make you grow every single time and avoid failure a majority of the time!

If you take the uncomfortable journey where you fail freely, you will find your spark. It will open doors to what your true passion is. Unlike other vacations where you are stuck going back to something that isn't enjoyable and fulfilling and don't get anything out of your vacation besides escaping your misery at home, you will come back from this book and maximize your vacation each day. The pursuit of mastering the most vacation time every day under your criteria being yourself is the game I play with myself.

Failing freefilled is the only way to have a world class Mental Beach Mindset that will allow you to live freely experiencing the present moment and guarantee you are free wherever you are. Over the last 8 chapters you have learned world class freedom and you are where you need to be right now!!! Whether that is at the Guadeloupe Airport, St. Thomas Beach, an Alcohol Addiction Center, A Rainy, Foggy day in New York City, or anywhere else in the world, there are a million beautiful places with beautiful people and everything is going to be ok wherever you are ☺

How Do I Shed My Fake Past Self Reputation When I Truly Find My Authentic Self?

This couldn't be more difficult for myself as I had so much internal self-doubt and insecurity as I started to become the "new real me." If you do recognize the difficulty in this question for your own personal self, that means you are starting to wake up! Because I used to try to impress the "Socially Cool Kids," it was easy to let a thought slip into my mind that people would think I was inauthentic because I was wasn't my past self. My mistake in the beginning of my journey was focusing my thoughts on external perception rather than what I thought about being myself, which looking back is basically taking action based on what someone else wants me to do and be. I couldn't live any longer becoming the "Best Possible Version of Someone Else." When it came down to it, I became selfish and started acting the way I wanted to every day without anyone influencing me and without harming anyone else. I wasn't being my true authentic self if I was thinking about what someone else would think of me being the freest version of myself. When I sat down and wrote the three most important things to myself, five principles to live by every day, and started taking action, I was able to find a resolution and come to terms with my mistakes and inauthentic actions I had taken in the past. I had shed the last bit of fear within myself and had finally unlocked the final door to becoming the best possible version of myself. My friends who I feared so greatly, wanted to hang out with my authentic self even more and respected me. Although it may be the most difficult, uncomfortable thing to do, attacking your fears in the present being your open, authentic self is the only way to be the best possible version of yourself. It is the only way to be eternally free from the negative energy used to convince your mind to push off the fears until later.

Once I Become Authentic, How Do I Become Good Enough For Myself?

I read John Wooden.

"You acquire a peace of mind, which is a direct result of self-satisfaction in knowing you did your best to become the best you are capable of becoming"

-John Wooden

And performed an evening routine created my amazing friend and goals guru, David, to make myself at peace to go to bed knowing I did my best.

Meditative Evening Evaluation

1. Did Today Matter?
2. Did I Accomplish What I Intended to Do?
3. Celebrate Wins
4. Capitalize on Failure/Learning Opportunities
5. Did I Enjoy the Journey Today To The Best of My Ability Without Restricting The Freedom of Being Healthy?

Action

Pre-Pave and Set Challenging, Achievable Intentions for The Next Day within your own boundaries ☺

How Can We Take Action?

Face reality when we do experience natural low points and create open and honest communication about what is bothering you with friends and talk it out! I wrote down everything bothering me in that moment and had a vulnerable, honest discussion with multiple friends about how to take action steps to move forward. When you surround yourself with the right people, they will be able to reason and talk you out of your self-doubts. At the end of the day, we all have a gift and we can truly do anything we set our mind to when we believe in ourselves!

Everything by setting boundaries between controllable and uncontrollable events is very important in order to shift wasted time and negative energy into positive energy improving yourself within your control.

And Stop comparing ourselves with other people and start comparing ourselves to how we can improve ourselves every day while helping others be more fulfilled.

Rise To Be more self-aware and listen by giving people our full attention.

When You Escape The Toxic Rope of Comfort

If We Attack Our Fears

Being Our Authentic Selves

Living In The Present Listening

To the People of The World

We Can Live Every Day

Carrying Out Our Life Purpose

Touching, Healing, and Educating

Through The Power Of Planting Seeds

Providing Love, Hope, and Support

To The People Who Walk Besides Us On This Earth

With Each Breath We Breathe

To Live a Life Where We All Can Feel

How Great This Day Is To Be Alive :)

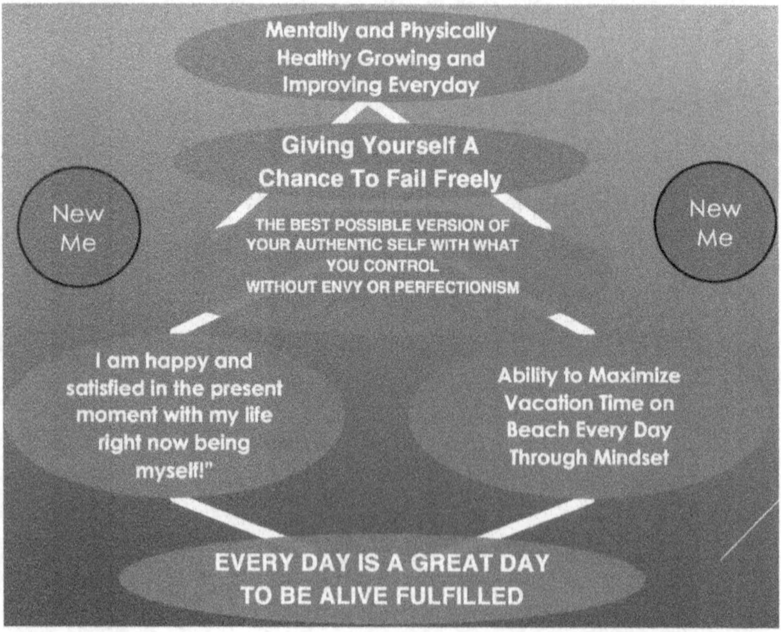
Mentally and Physically Healthy Growing and Improving Everyday
Giving Yourself A Chance To Fail Freely
New Me
New Me
THE BEST POSSIBLE VERSION OF YOUR AUTHENTIC SELF WITH WHAT YOU CONTROL WITHOUT ENVY OR PERFECTIONISM
I am happy and satisfied in the present moment with my life right now being myself!"
Ability to Maximize Vacation Time on Beach Every Day Through Mindset
EVERY DAY IS A GREAT DAY TO BE ALIVE FULFILLED

CHAPTER 10

CONCLUSION

It was cool crossing the finishing line at the NYC Marathon as an unofficial Guinness world record holder. But there will be nothing as freefilling as attempting to climb Mount Chimborazo after failing miserably with Gianna. Gianna had spent three weeks and her life savings to climb Chimborazo for orphans only to have an avalanche stop us from reaching the top, the closest point to the terrestrial stars. Once we get to the top, I will be failing freely for space with Bezos, Branson, and Musk. I don't have fear in 2018 besides the amount of people currently having their freedom taken away by someone who is unintentionally trying to help them Fail Down. I still need to cure food allergies, successfully climb down the India Venster Route on Table Mountain, and free the many I have failed down with. But that is going to make journey worth it. And I will embrace every minute like it's my last. I am going to spend every minute I am not pleasing and freeing myself to help free you so you can wake up and flex your freedom.

I have learned on my journey that we are really good at putting time and money into vehicles that will allow us to numb faster, yet we are really bad at putting skin in the game into our own self. By Not Putting Skin in the Game and Not Failing, comfort has allowed us to further numb out all of the problems through failing down. Hiding our problems under crutch pleasures has effectively broken the system, shattered our voices, and elected a president that built his campaign off of the hope of impulsive, instant gratification solutions to the current feelings of fear, greed, anger plaguing our country. The easy, wrong way out of this unfortunate situation would be to further numb out, hide our problems, and blame the president. The hard, best way to go about this would be to awake yourself using the "Failing FreeFilled" pill and go within yourself to be the best possible version of yourself every day.

Regardless of whether Donald Trump is exposing all these problems on purpose to force us to look at the ugly parts of our country or if he is a man who is enslaved by the unintentional harm positivity fallacy, it doesn't matter. What matters is that you move on and use the problems he has exposed and created to make yourself and others around you as free and alive in their own skin every day. Embrace this opportunity as a chance for you to wake up yourself and others around you to give this life the freedom and fulfillment it deserves. Because if we live freefilled experiencing each moment alive today, improving and growing every day, waking up mentally and physically healthy without harming anyone, we will get the last laugh and live a richer life. But you never know, he may be purposely inflicting harm on the world and our country in order to make America wake up from our numbness and confront our problems today so that we all have a brighter future together tomorrow. I am not praising the man, but rather spending my time on the only positive situation he has created, because I was numbly asleep on auto-pilot in 2016 when I voted for him, and I do care enough about you to write a book that will create more freedom than the amount of people he has stripped the freedom from and harmed. Donald, just like each of you is part of my journey. And I look forward to all of you living every day on your "Personal Freedom Mental Vacation Beach" like myself, because that is the only way life is worth living!

I ask you to ask yourself what it truly means to be you. I ask you to ask yourself what is truly important to YOU. I ask you to ask yourself what core principles do YOU want to live by each day. I ask you to look yourself in the mirror and ask who are YOU and who do YOU want to be. The only way to unleash your potential is to fuel your mindset through taking action on things that align with who you want to become. You are not going to find yourself through failing down with cheap thrills, but rather the true thrills with the people who allow you to Fail Up. If you are working at a steady job, I wish you the best of luck giving 120% dedication to your team and your boss and when you are not working I wish you are able to maximize freedom and fulfillment. If you are an entrepreneur I wish you the best of luck taking risks based on the frameworks I provided. I admire you for trying to change the world for the better, and if you do fail, I know it will be freely and will only make you smarter and stronger. If you are in college, I am so excited to see your progress. The opportunities you have to create meaningful relationships with amazing professors and create purposeful growth relationships with classmates are waiting for you to make your mark in a positive way. Get as uncomfortable as your fear will let you to become a better you! If you are in high school or middle school, I am confident you are going to change the world for the better with the resources you are equipped. I have a good feeling that one of you is going to create a positive social media revolution!! If you are parents, I hope this book allows you to create stronger bonds with those you have raised and put in a position to fail freely! All I ask is to not direct them in a certain direction where they feel strangled and waking up fearing every day disappointing you. Be more open, vulnerable, and communicate more frequently. If you are freshly retired, go out and travel the world at fail freely with those you love the most! If you are retired like my grandma, I hope you stop reading the NY Post and reading about how terrible the world is! You have created an amazing group of people that are fully prepared to embark on this journey and live freely and fulfilled.

To all who are pondering what to do in life, think about all the ones that are not with us anymore. Think about all the dreams of everyone in the cemetery that don't have a chance to achieve. All of the amazing things they were planning on positively contributing to the world will never be done. It is your turn to make their legacy last by spreading more freedom to yourself and others. They have paved the way for you to go out there freefilled and are rooting you on to make your days count. I can't tell you what the stock market is going to do in 2018, but I can tell you freedom is going to shoot up higher than bitcoin in 2018. The outer world is as ready as ever to make new connections, create more purpose, and create positive growth communities. You should be so proud of how far you have come on your journey, embrace your strengths and accomplishments and people will welcome you with open arms when you fail freefilled. All you need to do is Start. And then there will be no "getting back to reality" and 'welcome to real world", rather welcome to a world of being yourself, improving and growing every day, and making the most of the temporary enslavement that we are blessed to still be alive. I dream of a world where the question what are you doing after school, afterwork, or the weekend is answered by " I am going to be myself and enjoy my vacation."

If you truly want to make the world a better place, help yourself by finding your own limitless brightness. Lets write the next chapter of history failing up being our healthy authentic selves. That is the only and richest currency that will allow each of us to win the game of life together enjoying the journey of this beautiful world!

DISCLAIMERS FOR THE BOOK

BTB Free LLC Is not responsible for any suggestions or actions I recommend in this book.

This is a Book that may not be reproduced or transmitted in any form or by any means, electronic or mechanical, including photocopying, recording or by any information storage and retrieval system, without written permission from the author. Any use of this information is at your own risk. The methods described within this book are the author's personal thoughts.

Please understand this is not a book that will "get you rich." This is a book that will make you feel amazing and become the best possible version of yourself. You are responsible and accountable for your decisions and actions in your life!

ABOUT THE AUTHOR

About Brandon LaBella

Brandon LaBella is a globe-trotting visionary and recent cum laude B.B.A graduate of The College of William and Mary. His purpose is to use enthusiasm and positivity to inspire others to become the best possible version of themselves, mentally and physically healthy, growing and improving every day, and experiencing each day with the freedom to feel alive being their authentic self.

Due to life-threatening allergies to widespread foods and negativity, he came to understand the power of holistic health, community, and positive psychology. His education led him into successful opportunities at IBM, NASA, The Ministry of Tourism of Bali, and Fundraising Research with Ecuador NGO's for the US Government. His curiosity has led him to chase his self-worth by traveling to 45 Countries and 40 States and his determination has led him to become an unofficial Guinness World Record Holder for Fastest Marathon on Crutches at the 2017 New York City Marathon.

From a podcast on high-performing millennials to a nationwide book tour, Brandon lives to share his achievable optimism with the world. His infectious ambition has inspired hundreds of dream-chasers. And today? It's just the beginning.

In his free time, Brandon loves traveling around the world, playing golf, working on business ideas to positively change the world, playing sports, raising money for charities, and hanging out with buddies.

**NOW YOU ARE PREPARED
TO FAIL FREELY !!!**

JUL 2 4 2018

RYE FREE READING ROOM
1061 BOSTON POST ROAD
RYE NEW YORK 10580
(914) 967-0480